WELSH PROVERBS

WITH

ENGLISH TRANSLATIONS

BY

HENRY HALFORD VAUGHAN, M.A.

Also published by Llanerch:

A GLOSSARY OF THE DEMETIAN DIALECT
by W. Meredith Morris.

SYMBOLISM OF THE CELTIC CROSS
by Derek Bryce.

MABINOGION: THE FOUR BRANCHES
translated by Charlotte Guest.

TALIESIN POEMS
selected translations by Meirion Pennar.

THE BLACK BOOK OF CARMARTHEN
selected translations by Meirion Pennar

For a complete list, write to
LLANERCH PUBLISHERS, FELINFACH, LAMPETER,
DYFED, SA48 8PJ.

WELSH PROVERBS

ENGLISH TRANSLATIONS

BY

HENRY HALFORD VAUGHAN, M.A.

SOMETIME FELLOW OF ORIEL COLLEGE
AND
SOMETIME REGIUS PROFESSOR OF MODERN HISTORY IN THE UNIVERSITY OF OXFORD

LLANERCH PUBLISHERS
Felinfach, 1993.
ISBN 1 897853 24 6

KEGAN PAUL, TRENCH, & CO., 1 PATERNOSTER SQUARE
1889

INTRODUCTORY NOTE.

THIS rendering of 'Welsh Proverbs' was made by my father in the last few years of his life. Originally undertaken as an employment for leisure hours, the work grew under his hands, and it was finally his intention to translate all the 'Welsh Proverbs,' together with such of the laws and Bardic aphorisms as seemed to embody and give expression to the national wisdom. In many cases the original meaning of the proverbs was hard to discover, owing to the quaintness of their diction and the obscurity of the illustrations by which they were expressed. The English Rhyme, therefore, does not profess to be a literal translation of the British Reason ; it merely attempts to express the original sentiments in language as far as possible analogous to that used by the Welsh sages.

My father had intended to write an introductory essay dealing with the subject as a whole, but at the time of his death this was only just commenced. Until lately I have been prevented by other work from giving up the time necessary for correcting the press. As it is, my work has been much facilitated by the kindness of Professor Rhŷs, who has revised all the Welsh before it was finally sent to press, though where the Welsh is capable of various meanings he is not responsible for the rendering adopted. I am glad of this opportunity of gratefully acknowledging my indebtedness to him.

W. W. V.

Brighton, 1889.

BRITISH REASON IN ENGLISH RHYME.

1

Never will a judgment be
Without its contradictory.

Ni bydd brawd
Heb ei hadfrawd.

2

Reproach, the most strong,
Redresses no wrong.

Rhag drwg ni ddiwyg adnair.

3

To kindness from thy heart be kinder still:
To cruelty be hard against thy will.

Bydd fwyn wrth fwyn o'th fodd:
Bydd anfwyn wrth anfwyn o'th anfodd.

4

Till perseverance it doth wed,
Talent has a barren bed.

Gweddw pwyll heb amdynedd.

5

Death never would own,
That he took upon loan.

A ddwg angeu, nid adfer.
neu
Angeu a gyrch, ac nid adfer.

*B

6

Ugly monsters are not shy
Of their own deformity.

Nid oes wyledd rhag anferthedd.

7

He, who from sickness ne'er is free,
Of a relapse may fearless be.

Nid bydd adglaf o glafwr.

8

Evermore to weep and sigh
Not grief is, but calamity.

Adfyd pob hir dristwch.

9

Keen eyes are small gain
In a head without brain.

Llygad cywraint yn mhen anghywraint.

10

Malice ever hath part
Of a cowardly heart.

Nid esgar diriaid ag anhyedd.

11

Fit time, fit place, fit quality ;
These three are opportunity.

Tair amosgre pob peth :
Amser ; lle ; a rhyw.

12

He who would farm may undertake it
When he can guide a plough, and make it.

Ni ddyly neb gymeryd amaethiad arno oni wybydd wneuthur ei
aradr, a'i hwylaw.—*Laws.*

13

Nurture from three things genius draws :
Fortune ; acquaintance ; and applause.

Tri chynnaliaeth awen: llwyddiant ; cydnabyddiaeth ; a chanmo-
liaeth.

14

Each stain comes to sight
On a horse that is white.

Amlwg gwaed ar farch gwelw.

15

The greater the name,
The greater its blame.

Anghwanegid mefl mawrair.

16

From ripeness if it fallen be,
You'll find the apple by the tree.

Ni phell ddigwydd afal o afall.

17

These three things a lover to silence will bring :
A brook ; jealous eyes; and a cock on the wing.

Tri aflafarwch serchawg : cornant ; eiddig ; a chyffylawg.

18

We are merry, and please,
When well and at ease ;
But in sickness and pain
We essay it in vain.

Nid afieithus ond disalw.

19

Few fires have a rage
Which no means can assuage.

Tan gwyllt yw, ac na ellir ei arafu.—*Laws.*

20–21

A bow with twelve arrows, a sword, and a spear,
Are the three manly weapons it 's lawful to wear.
But with none can a weapon be lawfully seen,
If a slave, or an idiot, or under fourteen.

Tri arf cyfreithiawl : cleddyf ; a gwaew ; a bwa a ddeuddeg saeth.
Tri dyn a ddylyir eu cadw rhag arfau : caeth, a mab ni bo pedair
blwydd ar ddeg, ac ynfyd cyhoeddawg.—*Laws.*

22

Who cannot wrong by might and main
By stealth his wrongful end will gain.

A'r ni allo trais, twylled.

23

Three things no credit to their owners yield :
A ruling wife ; lean horse ; and barren field.

Tri pheth ni ddygant wr i gymmeriad mawr : ei wraig yn feistres ;
ei geffyl yn llymes ; ac ei dir yn ores.

24

If you honour pursue,
Make honour your due.

Ni chaiff barch, a'r nis dylo

25

A clever man his theft conceals ;
But cleverer he, who never steals.

Call a dwylla, callach a baid.

26

The weakest, plotting in his lair,
May take the strongest in a snare.

Fe wna gwan, o fewn ei garn,
Ryw hocedion i'r cadarn.

27

A wise man will hit
With the edge of his wit.

Arf doeth yw pwyll.

28

Be your pity but small
For the fool, who gave all.

Cas a roddo ei gwbl,
Ac a fo ei hun heb ddim.

29

The mean heart will contrive, at last,
On the great heart some blame to cast.

Y fynwes, a fo anhael,
A fwrw rhoi'n fai ar yr hael.

30

We're ne'er indifferent to sooth,
But dearly love, or hate, the truth.

Cas yw y gwirionedd, lle nis carer.

31

Three things will drive a man from home :
A house, which reeks ;
A roof, which leaks ;
A wife, who wrangles when she speaks.

Tri pheth a yrant wo o'i dy ; cronglwyd ddyferllyd, sawell fyglyd,
a gwraig geintachlyd.

32

Less dreadful the she bear, whose cubs are gone,
Than is a fool, whose foolish fit is on.

Gwell i wr gyfarfod âg arthes wedi colli ei chenawon, nag â'r ffol
yn ei ffolineb.—*Proverbs of Solomon* (*Welsh Bible*).

33

Timid care, and nursing ways,
Never yet brought length of days.

Ni cheffir hoedl hir er ymgeledd.

34

The doctor worthiest of his fees
Was he, who cured thy mind's disease.

Goreu meddyg meddyg enaid.

35

Mischance comes quickly to the weak,
And one good hap is long to seek.

Hawdd i wan gaffael anhap ;
A hir yw araws un hap.

36

Who quits not the smoke,
Must content him to choke.

A'r ni ochelo y mwg,
Ni ochel ei ddrwg.

37

Who hath the poet's genius? Who?
But he, that hath an eyesight true
To nature, and a bosom tender,
And courage faithfully to render.

Tri phrif anhebgor awen : Llygadd yn gweled anian, calon yn
teimlaw anian, a glewder a faidd gydfyned ag anian.—*Bardic.*

38

Not all the smiths in Venice can
Make arms to shield one timorous man.

Ni ddichon holl arfau Gwenethia arfogaethu ofn.

39

To gain a victory o'er the old,
You need be neither strong nor bold.

Hen hawdd gorfod arno.

40

Genius, aright, and often, plied
With profit, soon attains its pride.

Tri pheth a gynnydd awen : ei hiawn arfer ; ei mynych arfer ; a
llwyddiant o'i harfer.

41

The evil field
Will evil yield.

Ni chêl drygdir ei egin.

42

To the sands of Malldraeth
Comes Owen in state :
For the sands of Malldraeth
King Owen will wait.

Nid erys Malldraeth ar Owain.

43

What is the best thing, man can have ?
A life that's ever just and brave.

Beth oreu oll byth a'r wr
Byw'n uniawn, na bo'n annwr.

44–5

What is plenty
Will content ye ;
But the dainty, and the grand dish,
Are the rare and the outlandish.

Ammeuthyn pob dieithrfwyd.
Nid ammeuthyn llawer.

46

Your big trees cast shade,
   And your forest's unbeaten :
But no timber is laid,
   And no venison is eaten.

A arbedodd ei lwyn,
A gollodd ei fwyn.

47

Let genius, working out his thought,
Guard it with silence till it 's wrought.

Celfydd celed ei arfaeth.

48

Better the blusterer's outbreak coarse,
Than passion's fierce and silent force.

Gwell trwch nag arwyniad.

49

Three warrants remember on buying a steed :
Till the dew hath thrice fallen, beware of a fit ;
The moon will thrice wane ere of glanders you're quit,
And of warrant from spavin a year have you need.

A dan dri haint y dylyir bod am deithi march : rhag yr ehegyr dri
gwlith ; rhag yr ysgyfaint dair lloer ; rhag y llynmeirch flwyddyn.

50

We are never the worse
For unmerited curse.

Nid argywedda melldith, onid i'r, a'i haeddo.

51

Rare style, rare matter, rare invention,
Make good a poem's high pretension.

Tri ardderchogrwydd cerdd : godidawg iaith ; godidawg ystyr ;
godidawg grebwyll.—*Bardic.*

52

But one misdoer's one misdeed
A hundred into wrong will lead.

Yn ol anwiredd y naill
Anwiredd a wna eraill.

53

Three things there are for ever cold :
   The marble rock ;
   The greyhound's nose ;
The fireplace in a miser's hold.

Tri oer byd : trwyn milgi ; maen clais ; ac aelwyd mab y crinwas.

54

Free to each mind the thought of each,
And free to every thought be speech.

Rhydd i bawb ei feddwl, ¹
A rhydd i bob meddwl ei lafar.

55

The mill ; the orchard ; and the weir,
Patrimonial jewels rare,
Nor movement, nor division, bear.
Take them wholly, single heir,
And with thy kin their produce share.

Tri thlws cenedl : melin, cored, a pherllan ; a'r rhai hyny ni ddylyir
   eu rhanu, na'u cychwynu; namyn rhanu eu ffrwythau i'r neb a'u
   dyly.—*Laws.*

56

Not the gift, but the will,
Makes a gift good or ill.

Nid oedd rodd,
Namyn y fodd.
  neu
Deuparth rhodd yw ewyllys.

57

Better rough stones, whose hindrance oft offends me,
Than even slabs, whose smoothness headlong sends me.

Gwell maen garw, a'm hattalio,
Na maen llyfn, a'm gollyngo.

58

He, who runs, going on his way,
Soon brings his going to a stay.

Gnawd wedi rhedeg attregwch.

59

Depart his neighbourhood will not
He, who the inheritance hath got.

Nid asgyr, a gaffo trefgordd.

60

Three things may make a woman naught :
  A giddy brain ;
  A heart that's vain ;
A face in beauty's fashion wrought.

Tri pheth a wna wraig yn anniwair : tegwch yn ei gwyneb ; ffolineb
yn ei phen ; a balchedd yn ei chalon.

61

Make a falcon of a kite,
Of a clown you'll make a knight.

Haws gwneuthur hebawg o farcud, no marchawg o ddiawg.

62

Better of roebucks to be first,
Than amongst antler'd stags the worst.

Gwell blaen yr iyrchod nag ol yr hyddod.

63

A proffered hand, with open palm,
Will give the coward's heart a qualm.

Ni baidd llwfr llaw ehelaeth.

64

A conscience pure
Doth make secure.

Asgre lân diogel ei pherchen.

65

Some blemish mars man's human shape,
When man in spirit is an ape.

Anafus pob drwgfoesawg.

Aneirian pob diriad.
<small>neu</small>

66

Not the praying at morn, and at noon, and at night,
Is the service of God ; but the doing aright.

Gwasanaeth Duw yw gwneuthur iawn ;
Nid gweddiaw bore a nawn.

67

Just reason is the wise man's rule ;
Example ever leads the fool.

Athraw doeth pwyll ;
Athraw annoeth dylith.

68

A child, and only he, does well
To give, and then his gift to tell.

Rhodd ac adrawdd rhodd bachgen.

69

True poetry must flow, from tutor'd art ;
From natural genius ; and a happy heart.

Tair ansawdd barddoniaeth : athrylith awen ; barn wrth ddysg ;
a gwynfyd meddwl.—*Bardic.*

70

Where liking is not,
Of faults there's a lot.

Aml bai lle ni charer.

71

Old age will take us unaware ;
And lay us helpless, like a snare.

Henaint a ddaw fal hoenyn,
A'i dwyll i efryddu dyn.

72

Better be wrong'd with soft pretence
Than hurt by boorish insolence.

Gwell eniwed fforfed ffug,
Na sori'n wladaidd sarug.

73

Who flays with a flag,
Will of flayers be lag.

Nid hawdd blingaw ag elestren.

74

Who hath no good but good descent
Is man as poor as ever went.

Gweddwa unpeth yw bonedd,
Oni chanlyn rhyw rinwedd.

75

The fault, which we share,
Is a fault we should spare.

Cas a ogano arall am y beiau, a fo arno ef ei hun.

76

When the wise a comrade chooses,
The biggest often he refuses.

Na ddos a gwr wrth ei faint.

77

Silver or gold in full supply
Will make a truth of any lie.

Ariannoedd neu aur ennyd
A wna gau yn wir i gyd.

78

What Ancients teach ;
The Cymric speech ;
All memories of the good and great ;
These three must bards perpetuate.

Tri pheth a ddylai Bard eu cynnal ; yr iaith Gymraeg, y prif-
farddoniaeth, a chof am bob daionus a rhagor.—*Bardic.*

79

'Tis hair by hair,
The head grows bare.

O flewyn i flewyn
Ydd â 'r pen yn foel.

80

Who long doth wait,
And climbeth late,
Down cometh soon, precipitate.

A esgyno yn hwyr ebrwydd y disgyn.

81

Flowers before May
Were better away.

Blodau cyn Mai
Goreu na bai.

82

There is a cause, could it be found
For a pea lying on the ground.

Achaws i'r bysen fod ar y barth.

83

No horse ever foaled
But left hair if he rolled.

Yn y lle ydd ymgreinio y march, ydd edy beth o'i flew.

84

Wretches are by their gifts more wretched made ;
A cat's fine skin but serves to get him flay'd.

Y gath, a fo da ei chroen, a flingir.

85

Three columns rear achievement : purpose bold ;
Continual effort ; failures manifold.

Tair colofn barn ; eon amcan, mynych arfer, a mynych gamsynied.
—*Bardic.*

86

The nightingale's nest
For passionate zest !

Nid serchawg ond ëaws.

87

March will slay you ;
April flay you.

Mawrth a ladd ;
Ebrill a fling.

88

Ill words, that blight,
Are dregs of spite.

Gwaddawd gwyth gair blwng.

89

There are many friends worse
Than the coin in your purse.

Goreu cyfaill bathodyn.

90

A fault, where fault is, all can see ;
And base men, though no fault there be.

Pawb a'i cenfydd lle bydd bai ;
A bawddyn, er na byddai.

91

Fear quakes at the sound
Of a silence profound.

Boloch ofnawg fydd daw.

92

Better with lands alone endow'd
Than only graced with titles proud.

Gwell iddo a ddonier, nog a fonedder.

93

To every bird that hath a throat
His own is still a lovely note.

Hoff gan bob edn ei lais,

neu
Digrif gan bob aderyn ei lais.

94

If a man to battle ride :
If a lawsuit to decide ;
If to church at holy-tide ;
Full dearly for his life shall pay
The foe, that kills him on his way.

Tri marchogaeth a ddyrchaif fraint dyn pryd as gallo hwynt : marchogaeth i luydd a dadlau, a llan. Sef fydd efe yna teisbantyle ;
ac mwy fydd y gosb am ei ladd, no phetai ar ei wedd ei hun.

—*Laws.*

95

Believe no tale
Ere it be stale.

Na ro goel i newyddion, oni bont yn hen.

96

Be the danger grave or slight,
Its gravest mischief comes of fright.

Gnawd y coir colled o fraw.

97

Of all the birds that haunt the bush
The most audacious is a thrush.

Nid rhyfygus ond bronfraith.

98

A gentle heat
Will make malt sweet.

Araf dan a wna frag melus.

99

No heart will be faint
To its guardian saint.

Hy pawb ar ei fabsant.

100

A year and a day
Wean a kitten from play.

Ni chwery cath dros ei blwydd.

101

A servant, faithful in his part,
Gives to his lord a lighter heart.

Gwas da bronwala ei arglwydd.

102–3–4

Boldness only makes attack ;
Cowardice will turn its back ;
Manliness in him is found
Who plants his foot and holds his ground.

Nid calonawg ond a gyrcho.
Nid diarswyd ond a aroo ;
Nid ofnawg ond a ffoo.

105

Every hog can rip and rout ;
But to unravel beats a snout.

Pob twrch a ddadredd, rhaid dëallus i ddattawd.

106

The priest who shrives a family,
On life's good things a tithe takes he,
On death his mortuary fee.

Offeiriad teulu, ef a ddyly ddegwm y teulu, ac a ddyly eu daered.

Laws.

107

An ocean can
But drown a man.

Ni wna mor waeth no boddi.

108

In waterish ground
Will rush be found.

Gnawd, lle bo dwfr, bydd brwyn.

109

No name is yet known
So sweet as 'my own.'

Goreu enw mi piau.

110

That which below we mortals hate
Doth God on high abominate.

Cas dyn yma, cas Duw fry.

111

Who makes most haste
Time most doth waste.

Po mwyaf y brys, mwyaf y rhwystr.

112

Our hand has no stain
If it work to our gain.

Ni butra llaw dyn er gwneuthur da iddo ei hun.

c

113

Could I do miracles at need,
On offal I would never feed.

Petawn ddewin, ni fwytawn furgun.

114

The best use of a lock and key
Is that which opens and sets free

Gwell egawr no chynnwys.

115

If 'tis little you have,
It is nothing you save.

Ni bydd budd o ychydig.

116

A hundred kine for men as many
Are better than is one to any.

Gwell can-muw i'r can-nyn
Nag un-muw i un dyn.

117

A secret soon will find a vent
Through lips of the incontinent.

Can rewydd nid pell fydd rhin.

118

Who gives small heed,
Can judge with speed.

Buan barn pob ehud.

119

The circumspect
Must recollect.

Nid call, ond a gadwo yn ei gof.

120

Would you confidence know,
Take with you your bow.

Nid hyder ond bwa.

121

Disgrace for light gain
Is a villainous stain.

Gwae à fyn mefl er bychod.

122

Of all, that run, most sure and straight
Is the running badger's gait.

Nid diswrth ond byrhwch.

123

Longevity's blight
Is excess of delight.

Gwedy anrheufedd
Pyr i'n gwnai byrhoedledd.

124

The finger is sweet
When blistered with heat.

Melus bys, pan losgo.

125

The homestead of dry cows brings profit small ;
But less gives that, which hath no cows at all.

Gwell buarth hysb nag un gwag.

126

Better sickle than bow,
For the work it can show.

Gwell gwaith cryman no bwa.

127

Pitiful he, who, threatening clear,
And threatening all, makes no one fear.

Câs a fygythio bawb, ac ni bo ar neb ei ofn.

128

Revile not the meat
Which you heartily eat.

Goganu 'r bwyd, a'i fwyta.

129

The babe will grow out
Of his napkin-clout.

Tyfid maban, ni thyf ei gadachan.

130

Those, who always turn deaf ear,
When they're speaking, none will hear.

Byddar a gaiff gyffelyb.

131

Least in damage to the right
Is the damage done in fight.

Goreu camwri cadbyd.

132

Store it with heed,
Find it at need.

A gadwer, a geir wrth raid.

133

Knowledge to earn,
Hold as you learn.

A gymero ddysg, cadwed.

134

A horse, which eyes the growing hay,
Sees not the fence, which stops his way.

March a wyl yr yd, ac ni wyl y cae.

135

Nowhere a man's beauty lies,
But in noble qualities.

Glendid dyn yw ei gampau.

136

Such strength hath no side
As brothers allied.

Nid cadernyd ond brodyr.

137

Whome'er love leads
Remembrance feeds.

Cof gan bawb, a gar.

138

No hand that is slow
Will be true in its blow.

Llaw frys llaw gywraint.

139

Give a woman some praise,
And her worth you will raise.

Gwell gwraig o'i chanmawl.

140

A lonely dog will seldom fail
To make companion of his tail.

Canymdaith ci ei losgwrn.

141

A coward, frightened, to his fear
Will sell the life of the most dear.

Llwfr lladd ei gydymaith.

142

You need not speed, you cannot stay,
A down-hill waggon on its way.

Rhetid car gan orwaered.

143

A friend, every inch,
Is the friend at a pinch.

Y câr cywir yn yr ing y gwelir.

144

The hand, in which the hilt is laid,
Has in the handle got the blade.

A gafas y carn, a gafas y llafn.

145

The dress of Youth is whole and spruce,
Patchy the coat of Age and loose.

Dillyn ieuanc, carpiawg hen.

146

The ball of twine in outward show,
Within is but a ball of tow.

Carth gwaelawd y bellen.

147

Play disappears
When play'd in fears.

Nid chwareu, a fo erchyll.

148

Words noisy and grand,
And a mouse is at hand.

Dadleu mawr mynych, ac engi ar lygoden.

149

Consorted with one bull, that's black,
Five score black cows no consort lack.

Os gwartheg tywyllion fyddant tarw tywyll wrth bob can-muw
o naddynt.—*Laws.*

150

These three, the roe, the fox, the hare,
A greyhound was not made to spare.

Tri asgafaeth milgi : ysgyfarnawg, iwrch, a llwynawg.

151

The shelter, which a hedge supplies,
Outworths the ground it occupies.

Gwell cysgawd y cae no 'i le.

152

The cleverness is but pretence,
That swerves from reason and good sense.

Nid dedwydd ni ddyfo pwyll.

153

Better heed and skill should bring
To his office, cook, than king.

Gwell coginiaeth na breniniaeth.

154

The lightest transgression
Is keeping possession.

Goreu camwri cedwid.

155

Short of supplies
Is the army, that flies.

Ni chymmer llu ced, ar ffo.

156

The cat, that swings, has little hope,
Hanging will use him to the rope.

Ni orddyfnwys cath cebystr.

157

He forfeits shelter in high place,
Who takes his shelter from the base.

Colles ei glydwr, a gyrchodd ty iangwr.

158

Better a hovel's roof and wall
For cover, than no roof at all.

Gwell y'nghysgawd y gawnen nog heb ddim.

159

Of all, that can be seen or heard,
A cock is the most social bird.

Nid cyfannedd ond ceiliawg.

160

Honour to the good is due ;
And men pay it to the new.

Ni cheinmygir ond newydd.

161

Bold indeed has he become
Who with his message trusts the dumb.

Cenad fud, drud a' i cretwy.

162

Clothes that are fine,
Wantons, and wine,
I pledge you my life,
It is safe to decline.

Gwin, merch drwch, a gwychder, myn fy enaid gwiw, afraid ger.

163

The judgment is through ;
And you wrangle anew.

Ceintach
Cynghawsedd } wedi brawd.

164

No travellers hie
So fast as a lie.

Goreu cerddedydd gau.
neu
Goreu peddestr yw gau.

165

Three things plead our absence on highest occasion:
Sore sickness; a flood; and a cry of invasion.

Tri pheth a ddiffer dyn rhag gwys dadlau : llefain ac udgorn rhag
llu gorwlad ; llif yn afon, heb bont, heb geubal ; a chlefyd
gorweiddiawg.—*Laws*.

166

Better delay
Than harm by the way.

Gwell araws na mefl gerdded.

167

If tongues should but tell
What in bosoms doth dwell,
Each man that you know
Would to all be a foe.

Pe dywetai dafawd, a wypai ceudawd, ni byddai gymmydawg neb
rhai.

168

Bad is the way to travel on,
Which travellers all but once have gone.

Drwg yw y fordd, ni cherddir ond unwaith.

169

The boar, and the bear,
The stag, and the hare,
Are the pride of the hunter,
And choicest of fare.

Penaf cig hely yw carw, ac ysgyfarnawg, a baedd gwyllt, ac arth.

170

Where a secret grudge is strong,
The grudge will not be secret long.

Nid hir y celir cilwg.

171

The thorn, that could not pierce when quick,
When it is dead will never prick.

A'r ni wano yn ddraen, ni wan yn gippyll.

172

Of creatures all, that run or fly,
The skulking woodcocks closest lie.

Nid llechiad ond cyffylawg.

173

Though many paths be in a dingle,
All lead into a path, that 's single.

Pob llwybr mewn ceunant
I'r un ffordd a redant.

174

The self-same man, when sick, and sound,
Two men, and different, will be found.

Nid un anian iach a chlaf.

175

Your fame would you win,
By dying begin.

A fyno glod, bid farw.

176

In scorning crookedness allow
Honour to the crooked plough.

Goreu cloff cloff arad.

177

Winning from land and sea their spoils
The luckless for the lucky toils.

Diriad a glud i ddedwydd ac o for ac o fynydd.

178

Riches take wing ;
Honour will cling.

Hwy clod no golud.

179

Evil should but evil gain :
Good for evil is its pain.

Bid gnifgad gwyd.

180

Upon a fair half-witted maid
Many a wanton hand is laid.

Pawb a'i gnith ar gedawr ynfyd.

181

'Tis a cock's proper pride,
That good eggs be supplied ;
And that, when the light broadens,
He wake you as wide.

Teithi ceiliawg yw canu a chocwyaw.—*Laws.*

182

When sickness comes, and doctors tend me,
From busy doctors heaven defend me.

Meddygon cleuon i'm clwyf ni cheisiaf.

183

Better a patch,
Than a hole, in your thatch.

Gwell clwt na thwll.

184

Seats, where the life of life doth rest,
Are the stomach, head, and breast.

Tri thrigfa bywyd ; pen, cwll, ac arffed.

185

If an ugly old woman fall, breaking her hip,
The pity she gets is, ' How clumsy to trip ! '

Bai ar wrach dori ei chlun.

186

Long before it meet your eyes,
A trumpet you may recognise.

Clywitor corn cyn ni weler.

187

When the larder door stands wide,
You need not push your dog inside.

Elid ci i gell agored.

188

Nuts hardest in shell
Will be empty as well.

Y gneuen goeg sy galetaf.

189

Who ties up a penny,
Has not very many.

Clwm anghenawg ar y geiniawg.

190

You'll sicken quickly
A man, who's sickly.

Hawdd yw clwyfaw claf.

191

Thrice thrice-unhappy, who, chastised by God,
Denies Him, while he bleeds beneath the rod.

Gwae a gawdd Duw, ac ni's cred.

192

As doors quit not their hinges when they swing,
So to their beds will tossing sluggards cling.

Mal y try y ddor ar ei cholyn, y try diawg yn ei wely.

193

You're a giant, if tall ;
And a dwarf, if you're small.

Os gwr mawr, cawr ;
Os gwr bychan, còr.

194

When hatred's tongue strike's hatred's tooth,
They ne'er make harmony with truth.

Tafawd gelyn ar ddanedd
Ni chydsain a'r wirionedd.

195

Every dunghill dog is bold
When up on his own dunghill roll'd.

Hyder pob costawg ar ei dom ei hun.

196

'Tis oft our lot a shank to buy,
When we have bargained for the thigh.

Coes yn llè morddwyd.

197

No rebuke ever hits
A man without wits.

Nid da cosb ar ynfyd.

198

The monkey 's at best,
With a pigmy for guest ;
And a pigmy most sweet,
If a monkey he meet.

Cymwytach corach a simach.

199

When all a herd dies,
One heifer we prize.

Cu anner wedi praidd.

200

The skin, in which he first drew breath,
A wolf will carry to his death.

Yn y croen, y ganer y blaidd, y bydd marw.

201

A buffoon profess'd
Likes scurrilous jest
As well as the best.

Ni ddawr croesan pa gabl.

202

Let the thief have his fling,
Who thieves but to swing.

Hir ledrad i grog.

203

If a fever age befall,
With it comes the end of all.

Cryd ar hen, angeu ys dir.

204

When for football you've a mind,
Go ; but leave your skin behind.

A el i'r gware, gadawed ei groen gartref.

205

One lov'd with love intense, and true,
As thoroughly is hated too.

Ni bu gu iawn, na bai gas.

206

Who first his harrow had in ground,
Sickle in hand will first be found.

Y cyntaf ei og, cyntaf ei gryman.

207

Candid as he, who can allow,
That mice may have devoured his plough.

Can ddiheued ag ysu o'r llygod y cwlltyr.

208

Three things do no good 'till they're knocked on
the crown:
A wedge ; tether-stake ; and a lubberly clown.

Tri pheth ni wna les nes curaw ei ben : cyn ; pawl tid ; a thaiawg.

209

For believing, rely
Less on ear than on eye.

Coelia'n llai'r glwst, na'r golwg.

210

Those, who're slimmest at the prime,
Are the fattest in their time.

Gnawd corffawg o fain.

211

Good ale in a bowl
Is a key to the soul.

Allwedd calon cwrw da.

212

He complains not at all,
Who complains against all.

A gwyn rhwy, ni ry gwynfan.

213

Eat with princes when you may,
But with princes do not play.

Cydfwyta a mab arglwydd, ac na chydchwareu.

214

When your ox is most spare,
Best speeds he the share.

Pan fo culaf yr ŷch,
Goreu fydd yn ngwaith.

215

Reason is a wise man's rule ;
Reason never with a fool.

Na chais gyfymbwyll ond â doethion.

216

Like and like are rivals still,
And on meeting strive they will.

Pob cyffelyb a ymgais.

217

A log 'twill take
A fire to make.

Nid tan heb gyff.

218

Of Being there are circles three :
The circle of Eternity,
Where God alone throughout must be ;
The circle dim of Inchoation,
Where death is life's origination,
And man is toiling through the station ;
The circle of Felicities,
Where life doth out of life arise,
And man hath mounted to the skies.

Tri chylch hanfod y sydd: cylch y ceugant, lle nid oes namyn
Duw na byw na marw, ac nid oes namyn Duw a eill ei dreiglaw;
cylch yr abred, lle pob ansawdd hanfod o'r marw, a dyn a'i
treiglwys ; cylch y gwynfyd, lle pob ansawdd hanfod o'r byw, a
dyn a'i treigla yn y nef.—*Bardic.*

219

As it pains to refuse,
It is painful to chocse.
Yn mhob dewis y mae cyfyngder.

220

Right hand left hand's weakness knows ;
Friend can lightly friend expose :
On such friendship shame and woes !
Car yn cyhuddaw arall !
Hawdd i 'r llaw gyhuddo 'r llall.

221

No aid the feeble can supply
Except the help to raise a cry.
Ni ddichon gwan ond gwaeddi.

222

If to no strong law subdued,
Hateful is a multitude.
Cas cyffredin heb gyfraith.

223

The prudent are friends
Of making amends.

Dedwydd a gar ddadolwch.

224-5

Earth doth weigh
As nought else may:
As nought else rare
And light is air.

Nid trwm ond daear :
Nid ysgafn ond gwybr.

226

That your business may thrive,
Take a wedge, that will drive.

Gyru y cyn a gerddo.

227

A tiny seed
Will monster breed.

Bychan fydd mam y cynfil.

228

In his own cabin uncontroll'd
The wrangling churl is loud and bold.

Diau cynddadl taiawg o'i dy.

229

As lessens frost,
Is vigour lost.

Lleiaes rhew,
Lleiaes glew.

230

He, who would surety set at large,
Has but the debtor to discharge.

A arbeto ei fach, arbeted ei gynnogn.

231

We most receive
In getting leave.
Goreu rhan rhoddi cynnwys.

232

Chance has a place
In every chase.
Damwain pob hely.

233

The owner's stock its owner's eye
Makes abide, and multiply.
Golwg y perchen yw cynnydd y da.

234

Let the heart that will not glow
To a long, long slumber go.
Calon, ni gynnydd, cysgid.

235

Many is the man, that would
An ill-turn render for a good.
Llawer dyn a wna cynnyg drwg dros dda.

236

Every land, that eye can range,
Beside the native hath the strange.
Gnawd cyrchyniad yn mhob bro.

237

Lay your bashfulness aside,
When on embassies you ride.
Ni chynghain gan gennad gywilydd.

238

We call him not clever,
Who prospereth never.
Ni elwir cywrain, ni gynnydd.

239

To every family belong,
Patron, to represent it ;
Advocate, to protect from wrong ;
Avenger, to resent it.

Tri anhebgor cenedl : pencenedl ; a'i dialwr ; a 'i harddadlwr.

Laws.

240

Men thrive by sleep,
Not long, but deep.

Ni cheir da o hir cysgw.

241

Though all around spilt milk doth flow,
The loss is little to your cow.

Colles dy laeth cystal i'r fuwch.

242

No lawyer, fee'd, spins frivolous pretence,
As lazy servants plead for negligence.

Goreu cynghaws gwas diawg.

243

When a king takes a wife,
There 's a widow for life.

Cywala gweddw gwraig unben.

244

To his fellow is kind
A fellow in mind.

Pawb a gar ei gywala.

245

When the convivial eats his fill
Help him, convivial, with a will.

Llewid cywestach.

246

For the skilful, at one time,
Two works will make a pleasant chime.

Dau waith a fydd gan gywraint.

247

Some of good their choice will make ;
Full as many evil take.

Nid llai cyrchir drwg no da.

248

The part its whole will hardly fail ;
With the dog will come his tail.

Gyda 'r ci y cerdd ei gynfon.

249

Fear not to go back, or stray;
Where an old man shows thy way.

Cysyl hen ni'th attwg.

250

Skill earns, but cannot keep, the gold,
Which saving thrift makes manifold.

Gwell cynnil no chywraint.

251

For thy banquet throngs contend :
Thy meal of sorrow brings the friend

Cywrys am fwyd,
Carant am ofid.

252

Not a word needs a colt
To be off like a bolt.

Gormodd 'bw' ar ebawl.

253

No ministry tender,
But a sister will render.

Nid amgeledd ond chwaer.

254

Gentle be thou in thy game :
By thy jesting bring no shame.

Chwaräa ac na friw; cellwair ac na chywil yddia.

255

He, who for prudence holds repute,
Takes neither side in a dispute.

Ni chymmydd dedwydd a dadlau.

256

The cheek of pure virginity
Must burn with scarlet blushes three :
When her father's voice doth sound
' For thee have I a husband found ; '
When she goeth to her bed,
On the day that she doth wed ;
When, to meet all human eyes,
On the morrow she doth rise.
The cheek of pure virginity
Must burn with scarlet blushes three.
Fee for the first blush on her cheek
Their lord shall from her father seek.
Fee for the last blush, that did stain it,
Her sire shall give, her bridegroom gain it.
Fee for the blush, which brought their pleasure,
Bridegroom pay bride, his joy to measure.

Tri chywilydd morwyn ynt : dywedyd o'i thad wrthi, ' Mi a'th
roddais i wr ' ; ail yw, pan el gyntaf i wely ei gwr ; trydydd yw,
pan del gyntaf o'r gwely y' mhlith dynion. Tros y cyntaf y
telir ei hamobrwy i 'w harglwydd. Tros yr ail y rhoddir
ei chowyll iddi hithau. Tros y trydydd y dyry ei thad ei
hegweddi i'r gwr.—*Laws.*

257

Some are merrier than their show ;
Ice-bound currents laugh below.

Chwarddiad dwfr tan iâ.

258

If the beloved but appear,
Unbidden smiles the face will wear.

Chwerddid bryd ⎱
Hwarddedig pryd ⎰ wrth a garer.

259

A child will talk
Without a balk.

Iawn chwedlawg mab.

260

Sweet is mead, when in the pot ;
Bitter, when we pay the scot.

Chweg medd, pan yfer ;
Chwerw, pan daler.

261

A maiden will not hanker much
After a friar on his crutch.

Ni chwennych morwyn mynawg baglawg.

262

All the world is of this mind :
To those, that cocker us, we're kind

Dedwydd pawb wrth a'i llocho.

263

Twixt crown and eyes
Our fortune lies.

Ffawd pawb yn ei dàl.

264

Though saddened by his length of days,
The old dog with the puppy plays.

Chwareu hen gi a cholwyn.

265

Inveterate will be, and shrewd,
The memory of an ancient feud.

Hir y bydd chwerw hen alanas.

266

Plume thee not on thy employ,
Thou, that serv'st a piper's boy.

Gwas i was chwibanwr.

267

Friends divided still will greet,
Ere the sundered mountains meet.

Cynt y cwrdd dau ddyn no dau fynydd.

268

Only then the best you take,
When of best the best you make.

Nid oes o ddim ond fal y cymerer.

269

British frolic's soft and gay :
Saxons kill you as they play.

Chware Cymmro digrifwch :
Chware Sais angeu.

270

The last of the old
Is by sheepwalk and fold.

Diwedd hen cadw defaid.

271

The serried teeth stand close around,
To keep th' unbridled tongue in bound.

Da daint rhag tafawd.

272

While good doth last,
Hold fast ! hold fast !

Dalu da yn hyd fu.

273

Genius in his darker vein
Only genius can explain.

Y gyfrinach awenawl ni's gellir ei dadrin heb awen.

274

A stupid mind
Makes deaf and blind.

Dall fyddar pob trwch.

275

In hobbling, nothing, which hath feet,
With a gander can compete.

Nid musgrell ond ceiliogwydd.

276

The world will rail
At those who fail.

Gair dannod yw am un, a fethodd.

277

The hand, from which abundance goes,
Shall take again as it bestows.

Y llaw, a rydd, a gynnull.

278

Hold thee from the court aloof,
Where is judgment, and no proof.

Cas barn heb ddangosau.

279

All the pottage, sip by sip,
Goes from porringer to lip.

O lymaid i lymaid y darfu 'r cawl.

280

If one oath twice the lips doth pass,
The heart is bold by truth or brass.

Drud ganu deu-lw.

281

The hap, which I rue,
Is good fortune to you.

Ni ddaw drwg i un, na ddaw da i arall.

282

From its talent apart
A widow is Art.

Gweddw crefft heb ei dawn.

283

Hoards may fail, or scant their measure ;
Bounty is abiding treasure.

Goreu dëaint daioni.

284

Every mind some thought will fill ;
Every thought is good or ill.

Yn mhob dëall y mae meddwl : yn mhob meddwl y mae naill, ai
drwg, ai da.

285

He, that is bent upon departing,
Will do no good before his starting.

A fo a' i fryd ar ddebed,
Ni wna dda cyn ei fyned.

286

Need's iron jaw
Will crunch a law.

Angen a dyr ddeddf.

287

Teach the docile by a nod ;
School the froward with a rod.

Dysg ddedwydd a gair ; dysg ddiriad a gwial.

288

No risk has he run,
No prize has he won.

Ni cheiff dda, nid el yn namwain.

289

Pay not for your sport to-day
By your sadness months away.

Chwarëus yn awr nid chwarëus y' mlwyddyn.

290

Endless width and weight of stuff
Bunglers hardly find enough.

Defnyddfawr pob anghywraint.

291

Each sigh that you hear,
Look for a tear.

Ni fydd uchenaid heb ei deigr.

292

Oft on its coming 'good' we name,
What, e'er it part, as ill, we blame.

Nid äa drwy fal y del.

293

Jealous thoughts, which truth belie,
Will be true as prophecy.

Dewin pob eiddig.

294

Good luck, as of old,
To the saucy and bold !

Hap Duw ddewryn.

295

Alack that, with the best for choice,
A man should give the worst his voice.

Cas, a gaffo ddewis, ac a ddewiso y gwaethaf.

296

Better is the wrong prevented,
Than the wrong that's best resented.

Gwell gochel mefl nog ei ddial.

297

Sad lot, to breast the raging flood,
And then be smothered in the mud.

Dianc ar Glwyd, a boddi ar Gonwy.

298

The strongest, on a dunghill cast,
One night, unclad, will sleep his last.

Bod yn ddiarchen, a chysgu ar domen, a ladd y cryfaf.

299–300

The faultless is fair ;
But not faultless the fair is ;
For, for fair to be faultless
An event the most rare is.

Teg pob dianaf,
Odid dyn teg dianaf.

301

Every proverb speaketh sooth ;
Dreams and omens mask the truth.

Pob dihareb gwir ;
Pob coel celwydd.

302

None, but the crazy,
Give aid to the lazy.
Gwae a wnel da i ddiawg.

303

Be as skilful as you will,
Labour helped you to your skill.
Bydd lew, na fydd ddiathrin.

304

If an angel when you roam
Be no devil in your home.
Angel pen ffordd, a diawl pentan.

305

It costeth us nought,
To be good in our thought.
Diboen i ddyn dybiaw yn dda.

306

The child for that will never cry
On which he never set his eye.
Ni wyl mab am beth ni wŷl.

307

His servants 'tis the devil's way
Much to work, and little pay.
Drwg y ceidw 'r diawl ei was.

308

The treasure must be buried deep,
That shall for long its prison keep.
Nid äa swllt dan ddiebryd.

309

The dunce will not lack
A rod to his back.
Ni ddiffyg ffon ar ynfyd.

310

He, who of pleasure takes his fill,
Finds, that the wanton's end is ill.

Drythyllawg drwg ei ddichwain.

311

If the sire be to blame,
The son hath ill name.

Anwir difenwir ei blant.

312

Vengeance, though the wrong be clear,
Still must do its deed in fear.

Nid gnawd dialwr diofn.

313

Better to be dead and gone
Than for ever preyed upon.

Gwell marw no mynych ddifrawd.

314

He, who welcomes task and toil,
Rarely seeks a foreign soil.

Odid difro diwyd.

315-316

No pastime is found
As with hawk, or with hound.

Nid difyrwch ond milgi.
Nid digrifwch ond gwalch.

317

Better than the best will speed
What seems unlikeliest to succeed.

Annhebyg biau ffyniaw.

318

He is not sound, and sober too,
Who in one thing seeth two;
Yet oft he uses best his eyes,
Who seeing one thing two espies.

Gweled deubeth o'r un.

319

When you hear a compliment,
Think, a third of it is meant.

Deuparth parch yw arfer.

320

He who cares not where he lies,
In the end uncared-for dies.

Ni ddiddawr ni ddawr cwdd fo.

321

The hind and the fawn
Lie apart on the lawn.

Didryf ewig ac elain.

322

The good, whom calumnies oppress,
Quickly lose their usefulness.

Difwyniant fyddaf o'm difenwir.

323

Honourable place is that
Honourably laboured at.

Urddasoldeb swydd yw ei chyflawni yn gyfiawn.

324

Care and sleep
Their distance keep.

Dihunid a brydero.

325

A calf in name and deed is so,
Which can at birth nine paces go ;
And from its dam at every teat
By strength of lip draw milky meat.

Y llo a ddyly ymdaith naw cam, a dedyllu groesyn o'i phedair teth.

Laws.

326

The deeper the sea,
The safer is she.
Po dyfnaf y mor, diogelaf fydd y llong.

327

Murdered one day will he be found
Who never cares to look around.
Ys marw, a fo dibaith.

328

He only, who a town will rear,
Shall make a desert disappear.
Dinas a ddiffydd ddiffaith.

329

The friendless is game
To all, that can aim.
Preiddiai bawb i bob digarad.

330

Brave, to the raging battle go ;
God before thee shield will throw.
Aed lew i gynhwrf cad, duw a'i differ.

331

Seek not mischief's cause to find ;
Evil tempts the evil mind.
Adwyth diriaid heb achaws.

332
Those, who misery maintain,
Poor thanks from misery will gain.

Ni ddiylch angen ei borthi.

333
The neglected at court
Are a plentiful sort.

Gnawd digarad yn llys.

334
A house dog will not need your showing,
When a rogue is by him going.

Nid rhaid dangaws diriaid i gwn.

335
Those, who are villains on the sea,
Upon the land will villains be.

A fo diried ar for, diried fydd ar dir.

336
The feeblest arm
Can do you harm.

Fe all diffrwyth
Wneyd adwyth.

337
Let the weak one take to flight,
If pursued by man of might.

Diengid gwan erlid gadarn.

338
To be vexed by his love
Makes a kite of a dove.

Dig pawb rhag a'i car, os cawdd.

339
The warlike in mind
A weapon will find.

Ni ddiffyg arf ar was gwych.

340

A helmless ship without a sail
Is a wren without his tail.

Ni bydd y dryw
Heb ei lyw.

341

Our tenderest cares we ply to make
The rival, that our place will take.

Ef a fagodd a'i dirprwyodd.

342

We only then begin aright,
Beginning with the end in sight.

Cyn dechreu gwel y diwedd.

343

Before the morning is away,
Praise not the fineness of the day.

Nid y bore y mae canmawl diwrnod teg.

344

You ne'er will foreknow
A blunderer's blow.

Disymmwth fydd dryg-law ammhwyll.

345

He, who bestows on liberal men,
Is safe to find his gift again.

Ys dir, i hael a roddo.

346

For five long years the plough must clean
A field, which late a wood has been.

Tir a ddigoeter, pum mlynedd y dylyir ei aredig.

E

347
Best saint is he, who nothing knows,
And that unto his dulness owes.

Nid santaidd ond diwybod ;
Nid diwybod ond disynwyr.

348
What good e'er was done,
That was envied by none ?

Odid da diwarafun.

349
The patron of the family
No other man can claim to be,
Than he, whose voice will win attention
When raised to urge his friend's pretension ;
And he who friendship not to fail
Will offer acceptable bail ;
And he who will be fear'd in fight
When battling with his friend for right.

Ni wedd yn bencenedl, ond gwr a ymladdo gyd a'i gar ac a ofner ;
a ddyweto gyd a 'i gar ac a' wrandawer, a fechnio gyd a'i gar
ac a gymerer.—*Laws*.

350
Diligent heed,
And diligent speed,
Are, in a messenger,
All that you need.

Digawn da diwyd genad.

351
Anger all men can
A passionate man.

Hawdd yw digiaw dig.

352

Priests benedictions may dispense ;
But these will not make innocence.

Ni ludd dywyni ddiffeithwch.

353

He, that feels nor ruth nor shame,
Takes no loss by any blame.

A fo digywilydd, a fydd digolled.

354

Dexterous the hand is made,
Where'er the hand is often laid.

Cyfarwydd llaw lle y doto.

355

Between two pigs, both small and black,
You've time to choose, though time you lack.

Dewis o'r ddwy fachddu hwch.

356

He, who argues with the wise,
Gathers wisdom by replies.

Ymryson a doeth, ti a fyddi doethach.

357

Thy neighbour should be
A mirror for thee.

Drych i bawb ei gymmydawg.

358

If you wicked are and cruel,
Pins you'll swallow with your gruel.

Diriaid a geiff ddraen yn ei uwd.

359

Though to climb the risk were small,
In descent beware a fall.

Haws dringaw no disgyn.

360

None so bounteous are as they,
Who nothing have, to give away.

Hael byrllawiawg.

361–2

All things else in measure be ;
Measureless thy charity.

Mae dogn ar bob peth.
Nid oes dogn ar gardawd.

363

Better far the evil shown
Than the evil, that's unknown.

Gwell i ddyn y drwg, a wyr, no'r drwg, ni's gwyr.

364

No oath, ever made,
Could the jealous persuade.

Ni chred eiddig er a dynger.

365

Show a man for ever cross'd,
And you show a temper lost.

Bid diriaid dryganianus.

366

Woe for him, to whom hath clung
Ill report, when he was young.

Gwae a gaffo ddrygair yn ieuanc.

367

From many faults a man may sever,
But from his impatience—never.

Nid ef a ddiwyg dyn ei ddrygamynedd.

368

One malignant hour may fill
A whole lifetime with its ill.

Byr ddryganian a wna hir ofal.

369

In England men stare
At the king, and his heir.

Yn Lloegr drychion rhyedrychant unben.

370

Many a dog is better far
Than many human creatures are.

Na drygddyn ys gwell ci da.

371

A naughty boy, when you have foiled him,
Cries for the mother, who has spoiled him.

Rhybuched drygfab ei fam.

372

Knaves, that at home do nought but shirk,
In a strange house will ask for work.

Esgud drygfab yn nhŷ arall.

373

When a wise word 's out of reach,
Silence better is than speech.

Gwell tewi no drygddywedyd.

374

Whatever is, yet none may see,
Whatever 'tis, will slighted be.

Dirmygir ni welir.

375

Who gives us on loan,
Forbids us to own.

Echwyn yw nag.

376

Puss eyes the pond, and thinks the fish good meat ;
But has no fancy now to wet her feet.

E fynai y gath bysgod ; ond ni fynai wlychu ei throed.

377
Of all the birds, that guard a nest,
The blackcock is the valiantest.

Nid gwrawl ond ceiliawg du.

378
The merriest sight upon the road
Is a dandy with a load.

Mal drygfoneddig a' i faich.

379
The fox finds no scent
On the way, that he went.

Nis clyw madyn ei ddrygsawr ei hun.

380
A bad servant is a curse ;
And to lose him is still worse.

Drwg drygwas ; gwaeth bod hebddo.

381
A fall a fall is ; but a shock
It is to fall upon a rock.

Cwymp ar galed lawr.

382
Vainly is cold water shed
On the visage of the dead.

Bwrw dwfr am ben gwr marw.

383
Hard truth, that debt, unpaid for years,
Through its long owing disappears.

O hir ddyled ni ddylyir dim.

384
Better was his mind, that thought,
Than his, who by that thinking wrought.

Gwell dychymygwr no gorchwyliwr.

385

Other weapons all dismiss'd,
Take the best, your naked fist.

Goreu arf dwrn moel.

386

Come there will, despite delay,
Evening to the longest day.

Cyd boed hirddydd, dyfydd ucher.

387

If any, who doth title make
Land through ancestral right to take,
Four times shall trace through spindle-side,
The laws against his claim decide.

Pwy bynnag a gwyno gwyn, drwy ach ac edryd, am dir a daiar. ac
a ddyco ei achau ar gogail fwy no thair gwaith, colledig fydd
o'i hawl.—*Laws*.

388

To get a bad wife
Is ruin for life.

Gwae wr, a gaffo ddrygwraig.

389

In quickness all, by flood and field,
Must to the nimble otter yield.

Nid esgud ond dyfrgi.

390

You'll chide incontinence in vain :
Leaky cups cannot retain.

Bid anniwair dyferiawg.

391

In the language, which they hold,
Differ will the wise and bold.

Araith doeth a drud ni ddygymmydd.

392

'Tis never you'll see
Two Welshmen agree.

Ni bydd dyun dau Gymmro.

393

The very steel of sword and knife
Should have a heed of human life.

Dygymerid haiarn hoedl dyn.

394

Provoking he, who learns and learns,
And by his lore no knowledge earns.

Cas a ddysgo lawer, ac ni wypo ddim.

395

Death, that's unwelcome to the brave,
Is a blessing to the slave.

Da angeu ar eiddiawg.

396

There is nothing so brisk
As a wren on the frisk.

Nid sionc ond y dryw.

397

Living, or for the table dress'd,
The sport, a salmon gives, is best.

Nid mwynaidd ond eawg.

398

The poacher like the owl doth pray
That night may lengthen into day.

Eidduned herwr hir nos.

399

Most of the praise, for what men sing,
Depends upon the listening.

Deuparth cerdd ei gwrandaw.

400

Who takes the nest built by a wren,
Shall never have his health again.

Neb, a dyno nyth y dryw,
Ni cheiff iechyd yn ei fyw.

401

It never will do
To say all, that is true.

Llawer gwir drwg ei ddywedyd.

402

Hateful he, who harm intended
Never by after-sorrow mended.

Cas a wnel ddrwg, ac ni bo edifar ganddo.

403

Who buys, what is not new and prime,
Will have to buy a second time.

Pryn hen, pryn eilwaith.

404

The eagle on high
Stoops not on a fly.

Ni ddeil yr eryr ednogyn.

405

Suing to the man you hate,
Is a miserable state.

Eiriawl, ni charer, ni chynghan.

406

To gain the object of your heart,
With something cherish'd you must part.

A'r ni roddo, a garo,
Ni cheiff, a ddymuno.

407

Full of delays
Are intricate ways.

Afrwydd pob dyrys.

408-9

Nothing, as the steer, so wild ;
Nothing, as the ox, so mild.

Nid gwar ond ych,
Nid taiawg ond eidion.

410

Sickness, as sickness, much we hate,
And death, as death, eschew ;
Yet is it commonly our fate
To sicken, and die too.

Bod yn hir yn glaf, a marw eisys.

411

Few men alive
An answer can give.

Odid, a ddyry ateb.

412

In all things being at this hour,
Nought in being is, but power.

Eithr gallu nid oes dim.

413

Borrowing, when you cannot buy,
A little betters beggary.

Gwell benthyg nog eisieu.

414

The learned and wise
Give gentle replies.

Ateb araf gan ddysgedig.

415

When your right you pursue,
What is right you must do.

Ni dayly cyfraith, nis gwnel.

416

Yon old man, now so lean and slow,
In youth did like a lion go.

Ni bu eiddil hen yn was.

417

Birth opens our eyes
Without making us wise.

Nid ef enir pawb yn ddoeth.

418

An aunt, full of care,
Is a mother to spare.

Eilfam modryb dda.

419

Though Bible-oath vouch gold as true,
You'll try it with the touchstone too.

Da yw y maen gyd a'r efengyl.

420

Icy if have been December,
All the frogs will frost remember.

Dybydd rhew i lyffant.

421

To sue, and sue, and suit pursue,
Is but sickening work to do.

Dygas waith erlyn.

422

Let him, who nought for mother cares,
Learn, with stepmother how he fares.

Ni charo ei fam, cared ei elltrewen.

423

It is need, and not fun,
If an old man doth run.

Angen a ddysgi hen redeg.

424

Sometimes the spoiler his own prey is made ;
The hawk has pounced upon a razor's blade.

Mal y gwalch dros fin yr ellyn.

425

He, who a hundred foes can tell,
Shall count a hundred friends as well.

Cant car a fydd i ddyn a chant esgar.

426

One torch will not flare
So bright as a pair.

Gwell y llysg dau etewyn nog un.

427

To love, and then leave,
Is to love, and to grieve.

Dygn yw adaw, a garer.

428

He, who advice unask'd doth push,
At random fires into a bush.

Ergyd yn llwyn cysyl heb erchi.

429

No eagle so weak,
But he's strong in the beak.

Nerth eryr yn ei ylfin.

430

If but brave banners round assemble,
A coward's limbs begin to tremble.

Ergryn llwfr lliaws eiddoed.

431

A mother that works
Makes a daughter that shirks ;
And a daughter that lags
Makes a mother that fags.

Mam esgud a wna ferch ddiawg.

432

Each day more rife,
Light, Truth, and Life
O'er all things are their triumph winning ;
And thus will end this dim beginning.

Tri pheth sydd ar eu cynnydd : tan, sef goleuad ; deall a gwirionedd ; ac enaid, sef bywyd ; a gorfod a wnant ar bob peth ; ac
yna diwedd abred.—*Bardic.*

433

No bargain he makes,
No profit who takes.

Ni mad newid, ni cheiff elw.

434

Brothers in trade, or good, or ill,
Are seldom brothers in good will.

Mal dau eurych.

435

If a youth his promise gave,
Think it foam upon a wave.

Ewyn dwfr addewid gwas.

436

A thief within the house he locks,
Who stops his earth against a fox.

Nid cau ffau ar lwynawg.

437

Confess and honour Fortune's sway
Man must, unto the Judgment Day.

Gweini ffawd hyd frawd ys dir.

438

No oath, ever made,
Could the jealous persuade.

Ni chred eiddig er a dynger.

439

One year is our mother,
Our stepdame another.

Y naill flwyddyn a fydd mam i ddyn, a'r llall fydd ei elltrewen.

440

Any knot, but the fast,
Is a knot not to last.

Clwm eiddil moch ellwng.

441

Nor worth in blood, nor rank in state,
Gives title to be fortunate.

Ni ludd ammraint ffawd.

442

'Tis not for him, who flies his foe,
To choose the pace, at which he'll go.

Ni cheiff ei ddewis gam, a fföo.

443

Few things in sloth can servants match ;
But none their watch-dog sleeping catch.

Nid esgeulus ond gweinidawg :
Nid cywir ond ci.

444

Three things there are, which now and ever
A fool's laughter will attend :
What is good ; and what is ill ; and
What he cannot comprehend.

Tri chwerthin ffol : am ben y da ; am ben y drwg ; ac am ben nas
gwyr pa beth.—*Bardic.*

445

He, who loves ease, or money, or good fare,
For his own country has no love to spare.

Tri dyn ni charant eu gwlad ; a garo ei fol ; a garo gyfoeth ; a
garo esmwythder.—*Bardic.*

446

He, whose purse holds not a sou,
Will have an empty headpiece too.

Fol pob tlawd.

447

There's a folly to blame
In each sin, you can name.

Yn mhob pechawd y mae ffoledd.

448

Starting with staff in hand, the old
A third foot in his hand doth hold.

Trydydd troed i hen ei ffon.

449

The way that is the best to go
Is the way that best you know.

Deuparth ffordd ei gwybod.

450

A woman, whom the world doth blame,
Will but verify her shame.

Elid gwraig yn ol ei henllib.

451

The rush of the steer
From an upland is queer.

Rhuthr enderig o'r allt.

452

Famine feeds without a care
What to take and what to spare

Ni ddyddawr newynawg pa yso.

453

Of faith the best part
Hath its seat in the heart.

Deuparth ffydd y' nghalon.

454

Better the horse, who plods the way,
Than he, who fattens by the hay.

Gwell yw y march, a fo yn ei fforddwydd, nog, a fo yn ei breseb.

455

How great the want, which wells supply,
We know not till our well is dry.

Ni wyddys eisieu y ffynnon, onid el yn hesb.

456

Always from good to better state—
'Tis thus that fare the fortunate.

Gwell well pob ffynedig.

457

Hateful is he, who wills not good,
And hinders others, when they would.

Cas, ni wnel dda, ac nis gato i arall.

458

From God Himself cannot be had
What shall be good to him that 's bad.

Ni eill Duw dda i ddiriad.

459

Tittle by tittle ;
Stroke upon stroke ;
The wedge, be it little,
Rendeth the oak.

Bob yn ddryll ydd â'r aing yn y pren.

460

To your cat do not commit,
For safe keeping, a tit-bit.

Adneu cyhyryn gan gath.

461

Leave not your wife for one disgrace,
Or you'll retake her with a brace.

Gadu gwraig ag un fefl, a'i chymmeryd a dwy.

462

There is not a man
Can more than he can.

Ni eill neb namyn ei allu.

463

He on the fight has most to say
Who in the fight will run away.

Gnawd ffo ar fraeth.

464

Murmurs are the words we use,
When we love ; and when we lose ;
And when we've asked, what all refuse.

Tri achaws cyffredin sydd i alar : serch ; coll ; a gwrthwyneb.

465

Of flagrant disproportion
The herneshaw is the paragon ;
For the herneshaw Nature built
Like a fowl upon a stilt.

Nid anferth ond garan.
Mal y garan am ei ddwygoes.

466

Take no controversy with thee
To a smith in his own stithy.

Ymryson a'r gof yn ei efail.

F

467–8

The Law no other ox doth know
Than one, that with a plough can go,
And tractably true pace can keep,
Through virgin soil, or furrow deep,
Adown the hill, and up the steep.

Teithi ych yw aredig yn rhych, ac y'ngwellt, ac y'ngallt, ac yn
ngwaered : a hynny yn ddidonwryg ; ac ni bydd teithiawl oni
bydd efelly.—*Laws.*

469

A goat does not mind
If she show what 's behind.

Mwy no'r afr er dangaws ei thin.

470

To call him bold
Grudge not thy breath,
Who knowing seeks
A painful death.

Angeu garw drud a'i heirch.

471

In all above, and nought below,
His hock, the new-foal'd colt will grow

Tyfid ebawl o hyd gar.

472

Other mercy than his foes'
Shall of a man's life dispose.

Hoedl dyn nid gelyn a'i rhan.

473

The praise of what's dear
It is music to hear.

Melys geirda am a garer.

474

This you can say without dispute,
' He is not lying while he's mute.'

Ni elwir yn euawg, onis geirydd.

475

The prudent other gifts may scorn,
Grant him only to be born.

Nid rhaid i ddedwydd namyn ei eni.

476

The swift will overtake the game ;
But the clever make it tame.

Drud i ddala, doeth i estwng.

477–8

Resolute alone is he
Who his end doth clearly see :
And, sure as mountain peak is cold,
Will the resolute be bold.

Nid glewineb ond gloewineb.
Bid drud glew, a bid rew bre.

479

When born thou art,
Thou 'rt born to part.

Pob byw a enir i ysgar.

480

Three gluttons are there on the earth,
With feeding never satisfied :
    A city's need ;
    The ocean's greed ;
A lord's rapacity and pride.

Tri glwth byd : mor ; dinas ; ac arglwydd.

481

No country is known
That no hero doth own.

Y' mhob gwlad y megir glew.

482

Lions tawny in the hair
Any living thing will dare ;
But when lions' hair is hoar,
Lions lions are no more.

Glew a fydd llew hyd yn llwyd.

483

A horse be to the indolent,
A dog be to the glutton, sent.

March i ddiawg, ci i lwth.

484

God is too good
For a desperate mood.

Gwell Duw no drwg obaith.

485

On the leaf, where it doth lie,
A jewel flames the butterfly.

Gloynau duw gleiniau dail.

486

Praise, if but skilfully you serve it,
Makes undeservers to deserve it.

Gnawd o'i ganmawl canmoladwy.

487

If, two meals out of three, you fast,
You'll gormandise the third and last.

Dau bryd newynawg a wna'r trydydd yn lwth.

488

Price will declare
The thing, that is rare.

Gwerthawg pob godidawg.

489

What milk you from the udder draw
You gave the cow through mouth and maw.

Godroid buwch o'i phen.

490

Strangers meeting
Change a greeting.

Gogyfeirch pawb ar ni wypo.

491

An anxious heart
Must ache and smart.

Dolurus calon ofalfawr.

492

He, who best bears him in the strife,
Will still be best for peaceful life.

A fo goreu i ryfel, goreu fydd i heddwch.

493

Chaff you will meet
Where'er there is wheat.

Mae gohilion i'r gwenith.

494

To the Universal eye
Nothing is a mystery.

Goiaen a wel y'nghyfing.

495

The violent all
By violence fall.

Dywal, dir fydd ei olaith.

496

Labour alone to man can prove
That labour is a thing to love.

Ni char gwaith, nis gorddyfno.

497

Preach no sermons over meat :
When you worship, do not eat.

Amser i fwyd ; ac amser i olychwyd.

498

The wife, who all the day doth rest
Seldom of dairies has the best.

Ni lwydd cell goreisteddwraig.

499

Those who never leave their chairs
Have but scandals for their wares.

Hir oreistedd i ogan.

500

Few the tedious course attend ;
All will watch the crowning end.

Pawb yn y gorphen.

501

Death is gain
To those in pain.

Gwell golaith na gofid.

502

None with worse grace, than fools, submit,
When they have got the worst of it.

Ni ad annoeth ei orfod.

503

Officious kindness do not show ;
Stroke not dogs when by you go.

Gorlyfnu pen ci tra eler heibio.

504

A threat of your life
Is less keen than a knife.

Ni ladd gogyfaddaw.

505

To meet with suffering is to fare
Better than to dwell with care.

Gwell goddef na gofal.

506

Arm all that live on sea and land ;
One naked truth will all withstand.

Y gwir yn erbyn y byd.

507

Let it never be thy pride
In thy chamber to abide.

Na fydd oreisteddgar yn ystafell.

508

Let man respect,
If God direct.

A osodo Duw parched dyn.

509

No person is a citizen,
Who any of the three—
A woman, or an alien,
Or destitute—may be.
And never shall attain belief,
By solemnest word spoken,
Witness forsworn, or arrant thief,
Or monk whose vows are broken.

Anaddwyn yw alltud, a dyn heb ateb arno, a gwraig : a'r tri dyn
nid gair eu gair, beth bynnag a ddywedont: sef, crefyddwr, a
dor ei ammod, a gau dyst, a lleidr cyfaddef.—*Laws.*

510

Its joint the spit
Did nicely fit.

Da gweddai y ber i'r golwyth.

511

From scoundrels will be ever heard
Of better men an evil word.

Diriad a gabla ei well.

512

He is not sovereign of the land
Whom any on it doth withstand.

Nid ef gwledig, a orsafer.

513

A hopeless task with hope he faces
Who an old horse would teach new paces ;
And presumptuous is the thought
That he need be paces taught.

Dysgu gradd i henfarch.

514

A scar upon a warrior's face
Is a warrior's proper grace.

Gnawd man ar ran cynnifiad.

515

Seek not the paltry to requite ;
A spear will never pierce a mite.

Nid â gwaew yn ngronyn.

516

A heart that holds no noble fire,
A liver heated with desire.

Drythyll pob digraid.

517

A pendant, hung beside the head,
Will on the cheek its lustre shed

Tywynid greinyn i ran.

518

The wealth, its owner would deny,
Will never bring prosperity.

Ni lwydd golud, a wader.

519

They burn to be consumed, who burn
With love, the lov'd cannot return.

Gwae, a gâr ni garant.

520

He shows a wonder, who can show
A wound, from which no blood did flow.

Odid archoll, heb waed.

521

As joiners better thrive each day,
Daily the masons more decay.

Gwaeth waeth faensaer ; gwell well brensaer.

522

When boastfully and loud men cheer,
Disaster, or disgrace, is near.

Hydr waedd gwaeth wrth fro.

523-4

To the cheek will the heart
Its trouble impart ;
And the cheek will reveal it,
Though the heart would conceal it.

Ni chel grudd gystudd calon.
Y galon er a gelai,
Y grudd a'i maneg i rai.

525

The pilferer, who steals the egg,
Will neither buy the fowl, nor beg.

A ddyco 'r wy,
A ddwg, a fo mwy.

526

To miss and to mar
No mysteries are.

Esmwythaf gwaith yw methu.

527

Each stone, that in the well you throw,
Swims till it touch the ground below.

Nawf maen hyd waelawd.

528

A pledge can defy
The rogue and his lie.

Nid oes wad tros waesaf.

529

With the bad if we 're curst,
Let us think of the worst.

Drwg yw y drwg ; a gwaeth yw y gwaethaf.

530

There is no cruelty above
The kindness of excessive love.

Gwaedlyd wrth faint dy drachywedd.

531

The house, that has no child within it,
Is a house with nothing in it.

Gwag ty heb fab.

532

Better the bag, which holds a bit,
Than the bag holding not a whit.

Gwell bychod y' nghod na chod wag.

533

A thief had need
Give all his heed.

Bid wagelawg lleidr.

534

Little you'll sleep
When fast you keep.

Ni chwsg gwagfoly.

535

Mean is the court, which gives not rest
And food, but to the bidden guest.

Drwg llys, ni ater ond a wahodder.

536

First to start, and then to stay,
Is no profitable way.

Dyfydd dyhirwaith araws.

537

When leave of our own flesh we take,
Leave we many a pain and ache.

A wahanodd gnawd, gwahanodd ddolur.

538

The patron of a family
Cur'd by its leech hath right to be
Of hurts all but the perilous three :
A cleft of skull, which bares the brain ;
Bowel through gash protruding plain ;
A bone, of arm, or leg, in twain,
And fee by leech be none accepted,
His blood-stain'd clothes alone excepted.

Penteulu a ddyly feddyginiaeth rad y gan y meddyg teulu, eithr
ei waed-ddillad onid o un o'r tair gweli arberygl, sef yw y rhai
hyny : dyrnawd y' mhen hyd yr emmenydd ; dyrnawd y' nghorff
hyd yr ymysgar, neu dori un o'r pedair colofn.—*Laws.*

539

Two-thirds of done
Is once begun.

Deuparth gwaith ei ddechreu.

540

You can lightly employ
At man's labour a boy ;
But the boy never can
Do the work of a man.

Ni cheffir gwaith gwr gan was.

541

Help the nightingale to sing ;
To the falcon lend a wing.

Mal adain i walch.

542

Often is the wrong thing done
Where necessity was none.

Mynych heb raid bod ar wall.

543

Make not a sty
Of your bed, as you lie.

Na fydd debyg i hwch yn dy wales.

544

To call him bald it is not fair
Who still expects a head of hair.

Nid moel gwr yn araws gwallt.

545

Truer greeting is a smile
Than provisions in a pile.

Gwell wyneb na gwaly.

546

Nothing is so weak and vain
But it will a power contain.

Ni bydd gwan heb ei gadarn.

547

Of a game comes the best
When from playing we rest.

Goreu yw y gwarau tra ater.

548

The husband's mother does not recollect
What, as her husband's wife, she did expect.

Ni ddaw cof i chwegr ei bod yn waudd.

549

Scoff not at the light
For the deed of the night.

Gwatwar y dydd am waith nos.

550-1

Let the adulterer take his blame ;
But to the thief be scorn and shame.

Gwell cynnwys got nag un lleidr.
Neud gwell got na lleidr.

552

They choice forsake
Who bargain make.

Ni chynghain gwarthal gan ddewis.

553

Young men laugh all
When old men fall.

Am gwymp hen y chwardd ieuanc.

554

Let the stone roll on ; so best
Level it will find, and rest.

Rhetid maen oni gaffo wastad.
Treigl maen hyd wastad.

555

The hen of every bird is good,
If oft she lay, and well she brood.

Teithi pob aderyn benyw yw dodwy a gori.—*Laws.*

556
Winter's cold you'll ne'er defeat
With a lighted candle's heat.

Rhag anwyd ni weryd canwyll.

557
Friendly shoulders wear a grace
Wanting in a stranger's face.

Gwell gwegil car na gwyneb estrawn.

558
'Tis an old man's wisest care
To be remembered in a prayer.

A fo hen, arched weddil.

559
Not enough is he receiving
Who shall leave it, nothing leaving.

Nid digon heb weddill.

560
A ball upon a level way
Is slow to stop, and loth to stay.

Ni cheffir gwastad i bel.

561
Fools only complain
Of a wound giving pain.

Gwelius nid ddidolur.

562
Who did no work, no prayer hath sped,
No right hath he to break the bread.

Ni lafur, ni weddia,
Nid teilwng iddo ei fara.

563
Climbing ambition does not reck
That always climbing breaks the neck.

Awydd a dyr ei wddwf.

564

What a wholesome child doth leave
It is wholesome to receive.

Gweddill mab iach.

565

Those own no bed
Who do not wed.

Nid gwely heb wraig.

566

Three duties hard
Hath British bard :
Of truth a mystery to make,
If Peace and Happiness desire it ;
Dispraise to give for Justice' sake ;
And from its sheath his sword to take
If Law and Order shall require it.

Tri angen wrthun beirdd Ynys Prydain : cel gan orfod er heddwch
a lles ; cwyn anfawl gan raid cyfiawnder, a noethi cledd ar
ddifrawd ac anrhaith.—*Bardic.*

567

Freely he the cup will ply
Who sees the bed whereon to lie.

Hawdd yf, a wyl ei wely.

568

Hateful the wise, whose craft protects him,
While no good principle directs him.

Cas doeth heb weithredoedd da.

569

With the hour, which evil brings,
Comes the turn to better things.

Dyddaw drwg, hanfyddir gwell.

570

No dog so mean is, that you'll rate
His love no better than his hate.

Gwell cariad y ci no 'i gas.

571

A woman mostly will prefer
The thing, that is the worst for her.

Gnawd gwraig gwell genddi, a fo gwaeth iddi.

572

He ill deserved the summer's day,
Who with his scissors cut his hay.

A'r gwellaif y llas y weirglawdd.

573

To change and change brings no reproach,
If change perfection thus approach.

Nid gwaradwydd gwellau.

574

Who loveth the meeting
Merits the greeting.

Haeddu anerch yw caru.

575

The squirrel's gambol doth express
The soul of Nature's liveliness.

Nid bywiawg ond gwiwer.

576

Stingy Howell could disburse
Freely from the nation's purse.

Hael Hywel o god y gwlad.

577

Fling not your hook
At ducks in a brook.

Bwrw gwyddif ar ol hwyaid.

578

A hero is so
Before he can go.

Gwas gwraidd cyn no'i gerdded.

579

The dwarf, in stature like a child,
Like a man must be beguil'd.

Haws twyllaw maban
Na thwyllaw gwrachan.

580

Be she old, or be she young,
A woman's strength is in her tongue.

Nerth gwraig yn ei thafawd.

581

Though stale the sin, and still the blame,
Yet fresh and frequent is the shame.

Hen bechawd a wna gywilydd newydd.

582

If you learning forego
You never will know ;
And a deaf ear to turn
Is never to learn.

Ni wyr ni ddysg ;
Ni ddysg ni wrendy.

583

Better and better till our beard be strong :
Then worse and worse, our whole life long.

Gwell-well hyd farf,
Gwaeth-waeth hyd farw.

584

You'll ne'er, by fair or foul, contrive
To make a dead bee store the hive.

Er heddwch nag er rhyfel
Gwenynen farw ni chasgl fel.

G

585

Of all things that can coax and soothe,
None is as woman's flattery smooth.

Nid gwenieithus ond merch.

586

Take all quietly ; e'er now,
Hurrying has killed the sow.

Yr hai a laddodd yr hwch.

587

In selling, to the rich apply ;
To the poor, when you would buy.

Cyfoethawg i werthu,
Tylawd i brynu.

588

Were I as she but half so naughty,
As she I were not half so haughty.

Pan gaer mi hi,
Ni cheir mi ha.

589

A single grain
Were omen vain ;
But chance never lay
Five score in the way.

Coel can haden.

590

Oft man knoweth when he goes ;
When he cometh no man knows.

E wyr dyn pan el,
Ac ni wyr pan ddel.

591

In no verse find I a charm
That will make my hive to swarm.

O englyn ni ddaliaf haid.

592

A true-born gentleman is he
Whose sire and dam both Britons be,
With no strange blood, no blood unfree,
Nor blood of churl in either tree.

Boneddig cynnwynawl fydd Cymro fam dad, heb gaeth, heb alltud,
hebledach ynddo.—*Laws.*

593

Thou wilt waste thy indignation
On a deaf man's hesitation.

Bid haha byddar.

594

A fisherman's wife
Has a happier life
Than she who was led
A fanatic to wed.

Gwell i wraig y pysgodwr
Nag i wraig y gwynfydwr.

595

When evil all about appears
'Twill be a costly cure for fears
To move the house that's round our ears.

Symudaw haddef rhag drwg

596

Dry sticks with flame no peace will get,
If sticks and flame shall once have met.

Ni thangnef gwynon a goddaith.

597

A star in the sky
For your hook is too high.

Mal haeddu awyr â bach.

598

A covenant's might
Will conquer a right.

Trech ammod na gwir.

599

You 'ld kill the horse before his day,
Who nibbles at the grass of May.

Bid fyw march a gnith gwellt Mai.

600

Lean curs the liberal soul pursue,
Until they make him currish too.

Dilyn hael onid el yn gi.

601

Vain are the words of blessing, said
To bless an ill-deserving head.

Ni lwydd llad, ni heudder.

602

If hasty men a wasps'-nest seize,
They leave it for the mad to squeeze.

Haeddu ar nyth y cacwn.

603

As easy 'tis men's thoughts to bind
As to make faggots of the wind.

Mal rhwymaw gwynt y'ngwden.

604

When you wish to have fine wool
Do not a goat's buttock pull.

Ni cheir gwlan rhywiawg ar glun gafr.

neu
Nid hawdd gwlana ar yr afr.

605

If 'tis need which makes us sell,
'Tis for need we buy as well.

Angen a bryn ac a werth.

606

Apart will keep
Disease and sleep.

Nid cyd-dyun hun â haint.

607

Of dogs, which growl,
The hides are foul.

Ci chwyrnawg halawg ei bais.

608

Thy penny came slow;
In a trice it may go :
Think of thy penny
More than the many.

Bydd 'di gynnil ar dy geiniawg :
Chwip yr äa ; hi ddaw yn ddiawg.

609

Whenever any dog doth die
Some dog takes benefit thereby.

Hanbid gwell y ci o farw y llall.

610

A girl, though long the change may lag,
Weekly alters to a hag.

O Sul i Sul ydd â'r forwyn yn wrach.

611

You have no skill, with all your wit,
Till knowledge shall have tempered it.

Nid cyfarwydd ond a wypo.

612

The sparkling wine-cup should be spann'd
Oftenest by a prince's hand.

Gnawd gwin yn llaw wledig.

613

What many get, keep but the few:
Upon a gander rests no dew.

Ni saif gwlith ar geiliogwydd.

614

Old age, arriving, to your door
Diseases brings you by the score.

Can gwst gan henaint.

615

Unto a distance sees the eye
Of him, who utters clamorous cry.

Hir ei lygad, a wrthgrif.

616

Ten claws must be ill,
One beak not to fill.

Ys drwg y deg ewin,
Ni bortho i'r un gylfin.

617

The wain may creak upon the road,
Yet carry to the end its load.

Cyd gwichio y fen, hi a ddwg ei llwyth.

618

If on his own word faith be built,
Guiltless is he, who's steep'd in guilt.

Gwirion pawb ar ei air ei hun.

619

The wantonest of birds, that brood,
Is the wagtail of the wood.

Gwingdin y llwyn, yr aderyn serchoga'n fyw.

620

He, who is less of man than beast,
The bidding spurn'd, will share the feast.

Gwrthawd gwahawdd, a myned i west.

621

Better to hear our bowel squeak
Than feel a blush upon the cheek.

Gwell gwichio 'r coludd,
Na chochi 'r ddeurudd.

622

He timely will plead
Who timely is fee'd.

Gan fod yr achwynwr yn chwenych hanota yn fore, efe a borthodd
ei gyfreithiwr y' mlaenllaw.

623

A beautiful hue
Hath all that is new.

Hardd pob newydd.

624

Lightly with their anger part
They, who truly love at heart.

Hawdd cymmod lle bo cariad.

625

What is easy, you'll discern,
When easy into hard shall turn.

Ni wyr hawdd fod yn hawdd, onid el hawdd yn anhawdd.

626

Light work is that,
They like, who chat.

Eiriawl a garawr hawddwaith.

627

You'll easier keep your kine at home,
Than you will track them, if they roam.

Haws cadw nog olrhain.

628

Of the nine chases these to all are free :
The stag ; the salmon ; and the swarming bee.

O'r naw helwriaeth tair helfa gyffredin sydd : carw ; haid wenyn ;
a gleisiad. — *Laws.*

629

To every ear the horn is blown,
Save that by which the horn hath grown.

Ethyw corn heb ysgyfarn.

630-1

With God if allied,
You've enough on your side ;
And nothing can stay,
If God be away.

Heb Dduw, heb ddim ;
A Duw, a digon.

632

Set not thine own price so high
That men shall doubt if they need buy.

Na fydd ry fwythus lle galler dy hebgor.

633

Home on earth be but a road
To our heavenly abode.

Awn ir nef i hendrefa.

634

The tongue of any wind that moans
Will lap up all a widow owns.

Gwynt a lyf dda gwraig weddw.

635

Where the alders spring and spread,
The dwindled privet hangs its head.

Nid unnaws gwyraws a gwern.

636

Long cherished passions often tend
In wickedness to find their end.

Hir wyniau i ddireidi.

637

Bards, in all lands, and every while,
Have been call'd 'Bards of Britain's Isle' :
For, underneath this island's skies
Did Bardic truth at first arise ;
And never on another shore
Was comprehended Bardic lore ;
And never can on any ground
Its truth continue and abound,
Unless, above its bards and round,
The voice of 'Britain's Bards' resound.

Am dri achaws y gelwir y beirdd 'yn feirdd wrth fraint a defawd
beirdd ynys Prydain' : yn gyntaf, am mai yn Ynys Prydain y
cafwyd barddoniaeth gyntaf ; yn ail, am na chafwys un gwlad
arall eirioed ddeall cyfiawn ar farddoniaeth ; yn drydydd, am
nas gellir cynnal barddoniaeth gyfiawn eithr y' mraint defodau
a llafar gorsedd beirdd ynys Prydain.—*Bardic.*

638

Three things for hardness nature made apart :
Flint ; gelded-buck's horn ; and the miser's heart.

Tri chaled byd : maen callestr ; corn hydd hefryn ; a chalon mab
y crinwas.

639

No child's mother e'er is known
To nurse the equal of her own.

Nid maeth mam mab ei hefelydd.

640

As many bacon hogs will be
As are the salt pits, you can see.

Hwch o bob heledd.

641

If a huntsman praise his hound,
　Think it but a pleasant sound.

Gair heliwr am ei gi.

642

Better that too much should stay,
　Than too much should flow away.

Gwell toliaw na heiliaw.

643

It is fair to defeat
　Deceit by deceit.

Hiced a ladd hoced.

644

If an old man wayward grow,
　Set him right without a blow.

Gwell cynghori hen no 'i faeddu.

645

Never flows the ale so fast
　As when through a strainer pass'd.

Amlaf cwrw tra hitler.

646

A deal, that men say,
　The wind bears away.

Llawer gair yn wynt a â heibio.

647

The best is best but in its place ;
　No jewel wither'd hands can grace.

Dillyn yn llaw henfab.

648

Longing, longing evermore,
　Hearts are withered to the core.

Gwyw calon gan hiraeth

649

Primest increase crowns the cares
Of him, who keeps a stud of mares.

Goreu hiliadaeth gre o gesyg.

650

The old, long spared by death, each day
Their over-ripeness overstay.

Aeddfed angeu i hen.

651

A calf will not find, anyhow,
Favour with a barren cow.

Ni châr buwch hesp lo.

652

Hours bright and warm
Oft follow storm.

Gnawd wedi dryghin hindda.

653

Better take thought
Than make onslaught.

Gwell hir bwyll no thraha.

654

Oats freeliest sprout
From tubs worn out.

Da hil ceirch gan ddrwg gynnog.

655

Never of old age can die
A once rooted jealousy.

Ni hena eiddigedd.

656

When heirs of land division make,
Its home-close shall the youngest take ;
The cauldron that the food did boil ;
The axe that shared the woodman's toil ;
And coulter that upturned the soil.

Pan ranner tir, y mab ieuaf biau yr wyth erw athref, a'r gallawr,
a'r fwyell gynnud, a'r gwlltir.—*Laws.*

657

Pull the hairs out one by one,
And the horse's tail is gone.

O hoenyn i hoenyn ydd â'r march yn gwta.

658

A sword in play
Makes swiftest way.

Nid hoewder ond cleddyf.

659

'Twas Ann that I sought ;
'Twas a cold that I caught ;
While a quick-witted man
Went away with my Ann.

O'i haraws bum yn oeri :
Aeth arall hoewgall a hi.

660

Languishing to draw our breath,
Long, is but a lingering death.

Pob hir nychdawd i angeu.

661

Love is, at least,
One half the feast.

Hanner y wledd hoffedd yw.

662

No charm hath life our youth beside ;
And youth can but an hour abide.

Nid hudoliaeth ond ieuenctid ;
Nid ieuenctid ond ennyd awr.

663

To the muscular the fat
Is, as the ball is to the bat.

Mwy no'r bel dan yr humog.

664

It is nothing but fair,
Of one's self to take care.

Iawn i bawb gadw ei hun.

665

Lovers, when absent, cannot find
The sleep, that would be to their mind :
And lovers, when together, wake ;
For mind they have not sleep to take.

Ni bydd hunawg serchawg byth.

666

One good thing out of hand bestow'd
Beats two, that are by promise ow'd.

Gwell un hwda na dau addaw.

667

Much to take, and give away
Nothing, is an ugly trait.

Cas yr hwn, y delo iddo lawer, ac ni roddo ddim.

668

Of all a ram's length
His head is the strength.

Nerth hwrdd yn ei ben.

669

No match hath a duck
For messing in muck.

Nid budr ond hwyad.

670

Wealth oft makes a shorter stay
Than a fit of anger may.

Hwy pery llid no golud.

671

The wider we roam
The welcomer home.

Wedi profi pob lle hwyfyd i gartref.

672

Short be cut
Horns, that butt.

Da gwaith rhoi cyrn byrion i'r fuwch a hwylio.

673

Easier flows a song at night
Than a song by morning light.

Haws cân hwyr na chân fore.

674–5

God's revenge doth travel slow,
But to give a speeding blow.

Hwyraf dial dial Duw ;
Llwyraf dial dial Duw.

676

Opportunity too late
Comes to the unfortunate.

Hwyrwaith i anffynnedig.

677

The duckling swims for many a day,
E'er swim his father's easy way.

Nid rhyw i gyw yr hwyad hwylusder nofio 'r ol dull ei dad.

678

Nobles learn half their noble bearing ;
But half the pow'r to learn is daring.

Deuparth bonedd yw dysg ;
Deuparth dysg yw hyder.

679

A man is at ease
If a neighbour he sees.

Hydr gwr o'i gymydogaeth.

680

You'll find no bliss,
If God's you miss.

Nid hyfrydwch ond gyda Duw.

681

Brute of such a noble mien,
As the hart, is never seen.

Nid boneddig ond hydd.

682

A thing most hated by the wary
Is English spoken in his dairy.

Casbeth Owain Cyfeiliawg Saesneg mewn hafotty.

683

Set not thy hand unto a work of might,
As 'twere a makeshift for a summer's night.

Nid âi o'i gylch fal gwneyd hafod unnos.

684

Bold is the roar
Of waves by a shore.

Hydr fydd dwfr ar dal glan.

685

His instinct takes
The stag to lakes.

Addug yr hydd i'r llyn.

686

If a man of high degree
By baser man encounter'd be,
No compensation shall he owe,
Whatever baser blood shall flow ;
For Worse should better know his place
Than meet his Better face to face.

O bydd i ddyn iselfraint gyhydreg a dyn uchelfraint, o gwna yr
uchelfraint waed ar yr iselfraint ni ddyly ei ddifwyn ; am na
ddylai gyhydreg ag un uch.—*Laws.*

687

The trouble to please
Our beloved is ease.

Hygar pawb wrth a garo.

688

Our intellect doth weaker grow,
The further into years we go.

Bo hynaf fo y dyn, gwaethaf fydd ei bwyll.

689

Many, that starve in single life,
In spite of hunger woo a wife.

Llawer un a ddwg newyn,
Ac er hynny gwraig a fyn.

690

Rumours, that about us fly,
Are seldom altogether lie.

A fo hyborth, hywir fydd.

691

Woe to the man, who shall resort
With an old servant to a court.

Gwae, a ddyco ei henwas i lys.

692

A cock, when he's proud,
Must proclaim it aloud.

Tryw i fab iar ddarogan.

693

No one living is so well
As he for whom you toll the beil.

Nid iach ond a fo marw.

694

When your gold to crowds you throw
Smiles in plenty too bestow.

A rano i liaws,
Rhaned yn hynaws.

695

What unto sheets of ice are stones,
Lords are to men of flesh and bones.

Maen dros iaen yw arglwydd.

696

Three qualities in style secure :
Be it copious, apt, and pure.

Tri anhebgor iaith : purdeb, amledd, ac hyweddiant.—*Bardic.*

H

697

Bear pancakes sway,
On great Jove's day !

Crempogau a bara miod ddydd Iau fawr.

698

No easy job,
A thief to rob.

Nid hawdd lladrata oddiar leidr.

699

When the ox the yoke refuses,
Then the ox the poleaxe chooses.

Dewis ai yr iau ai y fwyall.

700

To him who without cause complains
Cause shall be given for his pains.

A achwyno heb achos, gwneler achos iddo.

701

True love being,
Bliss is seeing.

Dedwydd i 'r a'i gwyl a'i car.

702

The wolf, in field a noxious beast
Will be no dainty in a feast.

Mwy nog y mae da y blaidd, nid da ei isgell.

703

To catch the roe I have no chance ;
And yet I know him at a glance.

Mi adwaen iwrch, er nas daliwyf.

704

Take the wayfare
With the way ;
Love a youngster,
Like his play.

A garo yr iau, cared ei warëau.

705

Through the world you'll seek in vain
Two things passing milk and grain.

Llaeth ac yd
Goreuon byd.

706

Each, for his share,
Has his own care.

Ys id ar bawb ei bryder.

707–8

The wealth of all wealth
Is plenty of health ;
And it bides not apart
From lightness of heart.

Nid cyfoeth ond iechyd.
A fyno iechyd bid lawen.

709

Hood your hat,
Grease your fat.

Iraw blonegen.

710

To comprehend, man beats his brain,
What God sees plainest of the plain.

Pob ingaf gan ddyn ëangaf fydd gan Dduw.

711

Milk our childish age did fit ;
Flesh is manhood's strength'ning bit ;
Ale our drooping years will hit.

Llaeth i blentyn ; cig i wr ; cwrw i hen.

712

He, that large store of bread can show,
To look for milk may singing go.

A fo aml ei fara, tan ganu aed i laetha.

713

Of sin religion kills the core :
Good manners only film it o'er.

Crefydd a ladd y drwg ; nid wna moes ond ei guddiaw.

714

A wolf, though like the lamb he bleat ;
Still like a wolf the lamb will eat.

Llafar oen a chalon blaidd.

715

What came the last,
Spreads wide and fast.

Llafr pob newydd.

716

At Myddfal three things make a cure :
Honey ; work ; and water pure.

Tair meddyginiaeth meddygon Myddfal : dwfr ; mel ; a llafur.

717

He never wears apparel gay,
Who dresses brightly every day.

Ni wisg cain,
Ni wisg lain.

718

The hand, that wrought that work supreme,
Wrought it as easy as a dream.

Nid llafurus llaw gywraint.

719

Wouldst thou be a roebuck-hound,
Thou shalt make a greater bound.

O myni fod yn iyrchgi, ti a fwri naid a fo mwy.

720

Of his own shade
Is a coward afraid.

Mae ar lwfr ofn ei lun.

721

The price of failure is not less
Than you need pay for good success.

Nid llai gwerth mefl no gwerth ffawd

722

Men oft you see destruction meeting,
As if preferment they were greeting.

Nid llai y cyrch dyn ei laith, no'i gyfarwys.

723

To make your lover speak take these for choice :
An arbour ; go-between ; and cuckoo's voice.

Tri llafarwch serchog ; hafdy ; cog ; a llatai.

724

Fast his tongue goes,
Who little knows.

A wyr leiaf
A wed mwyaf.

725

It's life and carcase you'll combine
To tell the value of a swine ;
And of the whole one part in three
The value of its life will be.

O'r mochyn deuparthawg fydd y cig ar yr enaid.—*Laws.*

726

Let him, who does a deed of spite,
Expect the deed that will requite.

A wnelo drwg arhoed y llall.

727

Two that are good no taint will get,
However closely they have met.

Ni lwgr da ar y llall.

728

The further up the tide doth flow,
The further will it ebb below.

Po mwyaf y llanw mwyaf fydd y trai.

729

Not to complete is quite to fail ;
Flay thou the cat unto her tail.

Blingo y gath hyd ei llosgwrn.

730

Better have God alone befriend you,
Than all the armies earth can lend you.

Gwell Duw yn gar no llu y ddaiar.

731

Murder'd was he who warning got,
And he who warning took was not.

Ef a las, a gafas rybudd ; ac ni las, a 'i cymerodd.

732
Though riches shall perish,
Good name you may cherish.

Trengid golud,
Ni threinc molud.

733
Practice will ever
Make handy and clever.

Llawaidd pob cynnefin.

734
Never will lord a service proffer
To him who no return can offer.

Nid a cynnyg arglwydd i lawd.

735
You will not Fortune's favourite be,
The more for all your purity.

Ni ludd anniweirdeb ffawd.

736
If toil bring gain,
Pains are not pain.

Y budd a ludd y lludded.

737
To a chatterer always show
What you wish the world to know.

Nag addef rin i lafar.

738
One sin, allow'd within your door,
Behind it brings a hundred more.

Un pechawd a lusg gant ar ei ol.

739

Who feareth the fight,
Will be slain in his flight.

Gnawd i lwrf ei ladd yn ffo.

740

He, who would with the devil eat,
Must with a long spoon take his meat.

Rhaid llwy hir i fwyta gyd a 'r diawl.

741

From a fox you can win
Nothing more than his skin.

Ni cheir gan y llwynawg ond ei groen.

742

The child good or bad is,
Just as his dad is.

Mal y bo y dyn y bydd ei lwdn.

743

The man of learning heralds place
Abreast with him of noblest race.

Arfer yr hen eirfyddion yw cyfrif dysg yn gydradd a'r bonedd
uchaf.

744

Nothing warms as sunbeams may ;
Nothing chills like moonlight ray.

Nid gwresawg ond yr haul ; nid oer ond y lleuad.

745

He, who goes neither sure nor quick,
Is the devil's walking stick.

Gwr diawg llawffon y diawl.

746

Hold its way
Nature's play !

Elid rhyw ei lwybr.

747

Nothing is so smooth and fair,
But a blemish will be there.

Ni bydd neb llyfn heb ei anaf.

748

No memory quite
Like black and white.

Goreu cof cof llyfr.

749

Only a dog will lick the blade
With which his mortal wound was made.

Llyfid y ci y gwaew y brather ag é :
neu
Y ci a lyfa yr arf y brather ag é.

750

About his trousers what debate
Makes he, whose legs are hardly straight !

Ewyllys y gwyrgam am a'i lawdr.

751

Many will the claim pursue
Of that, which but to one is due.

Llawer am hawl ; un ei dyly.

752

He who has done what brings disgrace,
Homeless and crustless hides his face.

Llwm o fan, a tham o dorth, ni cheidw ei wyneb ys gwna gwarth.

753

When truths increase ;
When ill-deeds cease ;
When strife is peace ;
Gladdened and gay
Bards greet the day.

Tri llawenydd beirdd Ynys Prydain : elwydd gwybodaeth : gwellaad moes ; a gorfod heddwch ar ddifrawd ac anrhaith.—*Bardic.*

754

Fattening hogs can never know
Wherefore squeals the empty sow.

Ni wyr yr hwch lawn pa wich y wag.

755

To foot the long, long way, then seek out, late,
Some friendly shelter, is the traveiler's fate.

Hir hynt a chyrchu llawgar.

756

The owner of a town-house, first on fire,
Its two next neighbours shall rebuild entire.

O derfydd ennynu ty yn mhlith tref, taled y ddau dy nesaf a ennyno gandd'o ; un o bob parth iddo.—*Laws.*

757

Fools long stay on earth will make :
Ill-fill'd bottles do not break.

Ni thyr llestr, ni bo llawn.

758

The liberal heart discern you may
By generous dole, and gracious way.

Ystum llawgar yn rhannu.

759

If Pride before you take his station,
Behind you stands Humiliation.

Lle blaena balchder y canlyna cywilydd.

760

Where wit and lore together go,
A purse and purseful they bestow.

Alwar llawn
Dysg a dawn.

761

Of ills confess'd
The least is best.

O'r ddeu-ddrwg goreu y lleiaf.

762

Better the hunks of whom you can get speech,
Than is the liberal—always out of reach.

Gwell cybydd lle bo, no hael lle ni bo.

763

Where a river shall spread,
There's a ford in its bed.

Lledled rydau.

764

The one wise act, I've done 'twixt birth and dying,
Is, that I came into the world a-crying.

Bum gall unwaith ; hyny oedd, llefain, pan ym ganed.

765

The first to take what's not his own,
Would be the first to win a throne.

Cyntaf yn lleidr cyntaf yn frenin.

766

'Coward of cowards,' you may say,
Must be the man who hides away.

Nid llwrf ond a lecho.

767

An old cat knows
When new milk flows.

Edwyn hen gath lefrith.

768

Beware the kennel of a pup
Which a fierce bitch is bringing up.

Cenau yn ei wal a gast lem.

769

A coward, once he's known, will feel
The brutal stress of every heel.

Pob llyfwr llemitier arno.

770–1

The lore of books can teach us more than age,
And natural talent than the learned page.

Gwell y gwyr llen no henaint.
Gwell no llen pwyll cynhenid.

772

Half the room in hell 's allow'd
To good actions, vainly vow'd.

Ni lenwir uffern eithr ag addewidion da.

773

Curst he who forfeits his own gain,
That he may give his neighbour pain.

Cas a gasäo ei les er afles i'w gymmydawg.

774

Who stops but to hear Mass and pray
Loses no time upon the way.

Ni bydd llesteiriach y ffordd er gwrandaw offeren.

775

At thy soup-plate do not seem
Like a sow a-gulping cream.

Llympraw fal hwch yn llympraw hufen.

776

The oath of a thrall
Is no swearing at all.

Nid twng llw gortrech.

777

The man who breaks another's land,
A treasure there to hide,
Four pennies owes him out of hand,
And all the hoard beside.
But every hidden store of gold
The land will for its monarch hold.

Os cladd dyn dir dyn arall er cuddiaw peth ynddo, pedair
ceinawg cyfraith a gaiff perchenawg y tir am agori daiar, a'r
guddfa, onid eurgrawn fydd ; canys brenin biau bob eurgrawn.

Laws.

778

Think, e'er thou sell thy house and ground,
Where then a dwelling will be found.

Y dyn a wertho ei dy,
Yn mha wlad y ceiff lletty.

779

When healthy girls reject their food,
The reason is more strong than good.

Llewid bwyd, ni bo beichiawg.

780

The profit from ill
Is soon of the past ;
But the good of the good
Will eternally last.

Lles dihirwch yn ddiflannawl ;
Lles cywirdeb yn dragywyddawl.

781

Your faith will be but ill bestow'd
On friends you make upon the road.

Car llwybrawd annilys.

782

Giddypate you'll never see
With old Silvertop agree.

Llwyd ac ynfyd ni ddygymmydd.

783

When blossoms on the elm appear,
Sevenfold fruitage crowns the year.

Pan fo llwyf yn ei blodau,
Blwyddyn y saith ffrwythlondeb.

784

The stone of Ceti weighs a load
For any wain on any road.

Llwyth maen Bryn Ceti.

785

Better to land a water-snake,
Than on an eel your hook to break.

Gwell yw dal llyfrothen na cholli bach.

786

Anger and frenzy mean the same ;
One devil with a double name.

Llid ac ynfydrwydd, dau enw i'r un diawl.

787

The frogs, which lie in ice-bound ponds,
Are not too free to feel their bonds.

Diffaith llyffant dan iâ.

788

A pledge doth lie
Beneath God's eye.

Llygad Duw ar adneu.

789

The German, Breton, and the Gael
Mingled pure bardic truth with bale ;
And therefore German, Gael, and Breton
Have lost the truth, their hands they set on.

Tair cenedl a lygrasant, a fu ganddynt ar ddysg o farddoniaeth
beirdd Ynys Prydain drwy gymysg oferbwyll ; ac o hyny a'i
collasant ; y Gwyddelod, Cymry Llydaw, a'r Ellmyn.

790

The furze its prickles well bestows,
To guard the brilliant bloom it shows.

Hardd blodau eithin ; eithr y' mhlith drain llymion y tyfant.

791

When the river's flood is highest,
Calm and sunshine then are nighest.

Llif yn afon, hinon fydd.

792

The cat, that oft one beard hath lick'd
Can by no other beard be trick'd.

E wyr y gâth pa farf â lŷf.

793

Liquor upon the wise bestow
And all the wiser he will grow.

Dyro lyn i ddoeth, ef a fydd ddoethach.

794

The fox knows quite as well as Hodge
On which side his fat ganders lodge.

Gwyr y cadnaw yn ddigawn da,
Pa le mae 'r gwyddau yn llettya.

795

The dream is bright
That 's dream'd in light.

Goleu freuddwyd a welir liw dydd.

796

Show not the milk your cow hath shed,
But show the calf which it hath bred.

Dangaws y llo, ac na ddangaws y llaeth.

797

Temper away,
Ill is the play.

Ys drwg mitawr,
O bei litawr.

798

Who fondles him, a child can tell ;
But no child knows who loves him well.

Ef a edwyn mab, a'i llawch ; ac nid edwyn mab a'i car.

799

Fleshfallen and tired
Is the ox, which is hired.

Llwm ych llog.

800

He, who would peaceful days achieve,
Must first of his own tongue ask leave.

A fyno heddwch, gofyned genad ei dafawd.

801

'Tis well, it should be shipman's mind,
In water his own ship to find.

Ceisied pawb ddwfr i'w long.

802

My best word of the bush be said,
Which shelter gives to me, and shade.

Goreu llwyn, un a'm cysgoto.

803

Never yet corrupt was found
A puddle, standing on the ground.

Ni butra llynwyn.

804

To knowledge handmaids three belong :
The book ; the specimen ; the song.

Tri gweinyddion gwybodaeth : can ; arwydd ; a llythyr.

805

How long the pedigree, or short,
It matters not in wisdom's court.

Bonedd mawr yw y peth lleiaf yn llys doethineb.

806

No botanist, that ever wrote,
Had half the knowledge of a goat.

Nid llyseuwraig ond gafr.

807

Coin no more in purses lingers
Than an eel between the fingers.

Llyswen mewn dwrn yw arian.

808

In long voyages there must be
The danger of being drowned at sea

Hir lyngeswriaeth i fawdd.

809

Give a whistle to a boy ;
To manhood be his plough a toy.

Hwiban i faban ; arad i wr.

810

In courts still better is a friend
Than gold at every finger's end.

Gwell car yn llys
Nog aur ar fys.

811

Good is his due
Who good doth do.

A wnel mad, mad a ddyly.

812

Light and short the task of him
Who a duckling taught to swim.

Moch dysg nawf mab hwyad.

813

In remembrance long will be
What a child shall hear, or see.

Da yw cof mab.

814

Better the broker that can sell
Than he that does but purchase well.

Gwell marchwr gwerthu nog un prynu.

815

No grasp will avail
With an eel, by the tail.

Dala llyswen erbyn ei llyw.

816

None, brutal in mind,
To children are kind.

Nid mabgar ond difilain.

817

The smith by hand ;
The hind on land ;
The bard with memory and wit ;
These three have done most benefit.

Tri madfanogion byd : bardd ; fferyllt ; ac ammaeth.

818

Pardon a Briton in his mood,
Of thinking none but Britons good.

Ni mad un, ni bu Gymro.

819

The snow of March which crowns a stone
Is white at morn, at noon is gone ;
And such my hope, which early shone.

Mal eiry Mawrth ar ben maen.

820

No tale you can weave
Will deceivers deceive,
Like the tale you believe.

Mataf gil gwired.

821

They go with toil who slowly wend :
Hard earns the snail his journey's end.

Malaen a ddyly ei daith.

822

Hinds to guide, and work to measure,
Is no task for monkish leisure.

Nid mynechtid maeroni.

823

A skilful general fights can win
Upon a sorry steed, and thin.

Achub maes mawr â dryg farch.

824

While of their load the hound his bowels rid,
Off went the hare, and in the wood was hid.

Tra bo y ci yn maesa ydd â 'r geinach i'r coed.

825

To rear him thou hast nothing scanted ;
And by him be thou now supplanted.

Neu'r fegaist a'th ddirprwy.

826

Slow is the thick ;
The spare is quick.

Gnawd buan o fain.

827

Folly would have Wisdom's eyes,
Could she measure her own size.

Ni wyl ynfydrwydd ei faint.

828

Any one you may suppose
To know what everybody knows

Da gwyr mal pawb.

829

Off like the wind flies woman's word,
As like the wind let it be heard.

Gair gwraig mal gwynt y cychwyn.

830

The farmer on a grassy wold
Should have no parlour, but his fold.

Cell maeronwr ei fuarth.

831

The inconsiderate, if he see
Thy finger, will ask it of thee.

Dangaws dy fys i falawg, yntau a'i heirch yn gwbl.

832

While preying larks the mole-hill try,
The hawk's wing flutters in the sky.

Pan fo meilierydd ar ben maluria, y bydd esgud asgell gwipia.

833

Let him, who claims a living thing,
His left hand lay on its right ear ;
His right hand to the relic bring ;
And so his title let him swear.

Pwy bynnag a fyno ddamdwng ar yr eiddaw, fal hyn y dyly ei
   ddamdwng : os anifel a ddamdwng, damdynged a'i law asswy
   ar y glust ddeau i'r anifel, a'r llaw ddeau ar y crair.—*Laws.*

834

Slow is the fire for porridge meet ;
To flummery give the lightning's heat.

Malldan dan uwd, mellten dan lymry.

835

With meal first fill
First sack at mill.

Cyntaf i'r felin biau malu.

836

The name of wife is only due
To her who is a mother too.

Nid gweddi ond mam.

837

Rage drives not its best weapon home :
The maddening boar's tooth gnashes foam.

Mal baedd yn malu ewyn.

838

Better a mother's purse and coins
Than sire's blue blood from princely loins.

Gwell mam godawg no thad rhieddawg.

839

To abide, no onset worse is,
Than a mother's, when she nurses.

Rhuthr mammaeth.

840

Or e'er we know
We must discern,
And, skill to show,
We skill must earn.

Ni wyr, ni welodd :
Ni feidr, ni ddysg.

841

He in the fight hath met mishap
Who hies him to his mother's lap.

Ceisied asgre ei fam, a gollo.

842

Many a kiss the child doth take
Is given for the nurse's sake.

O achaws y fammaeth y cusenir y mab.

843

When sweetest scent our sense hath met
We think upon the violet.

Mor beraidd a'r mill.

844

Each several part make fine and true,
And the whole is handsome too.

Manol pob rhan ;
Hardd y cyfan.

845

'Mid all the forms of human vest
A mantle covers you the best.

Goreu un tudded mantell.

846

Small is the grain of seed, that brings
Into being greatest things.

Bach hedyn pob mawredd.

847

Tractable for human need
Is no creature, as the steed.

Nid rhywiawg ond march.

848

Childhood's hands their lesson take
In handicraft without a shake.

Ni chryn llaw ar fabddysg.

849

Nothing that is dead will be
Long allowed within the sea.

Ni ad y mor marwolus ynddo.

850

Misfortune knows not innocence from sins,
Of sheep and lamb one market sells the skin·

Can ebrwydded, yn y farchnad,
Croen yr oen a chroen y ddafad.

851

Things shut in earth through earth break way,
But dead men in that prison stay.

Pob peth a ddaw trwy'r ddaiar,
Ond y marw, mawr ei garchar.

852

When cause, effect, and means are throughly known,
Man shall all ill, disease, and death, disown ;
And that day dawns on realms of bliss alone.

O ddeall tripheth y bydd difant a gortrech ar bob drwg a marw :
ansawdd ; achaws ; a pheiriant ; ac hyn a geir yn y gwynfyd.

Bardic.

853

No one need care
Of the dead to beware.

A fo marw, ni ymogelir.

854

To lie beneath your horse's hoof
Is of good riding sorry proof.

Cais marchawg da dan draed ei farch.

855

Unwelcome he to merchants' eyes
Who cheapens all, but nothing buys.

Cas a fasgnacho bob peth, ac heb brynu dim.

856-7

The good and just are great ; and small
Those, who pretend to greatness, all.

Nid mawr ond cyfiawn.
Bach pob dyn, a dybio ei hun yn fawr.

858

He hangs the pony's thief to-day
Who rode, last night, the horse away.

Marchleidr a grog y corleidr.

859

With zeal will he your errand do
Who in it sees his profit too.

Ni fawrâa neges,
Ni ragwyl ei les.

860

For good, that's done against his will,
The man, you serve, will thank you ill.

Ni fawr ddiolchir rhodd gymhell.

861

If wisely borne, thy first success
God will enlarge to happiness.

Bid doeth dedwydd,
Duw a'i mawr.

862

He who a great crime can commit,
By a big oath will cover it.

A wnel mawrddrwg a rydd mawrllw.

863

The Palace Judge's place so high
Is, that unhousel'd if he die,
His dwellinghouse, despite his end,
Unto his children shall descend.

Un dyn ni ddyly ei dy fod yn farwdy, cyd boed marw heb gym-
mun, yngnad llys.—*Laws.*

864

For all we buy we dearly pay,
And all we sell we give away.

Mawr werth pob newid ;
Bychan werth pob prid.

865

When just thy self-esteem shall be,
Great God himself will warrant thee.

Barn arnat dy hun yn gyfiawn, a Duw a 'th fechnia.

866

A sunny June
Brings harvest soon.

Myhefin heulawg a wna medel mochddwyreawg.

867

No bounty is bounty, that seeketh some gain :
No wisdom is wisdom, that follows some pain :
No thing is the same thing, to ruin when gone :
Nor a world without knowledge, a world to live on.

Nid hael hael ar fedr cael ced :
Nid call call wedi colled :
Nid dim dim diddym od aeth :
Nid byd byd heb wybodaeth.

868

Down with fatigue you will not drop,
Reaping a needy farmer's crop.

Hawdd medi erw anghenawg.

869

Pride is but an intoxication
Wrought by thy dregs, hallucination !

Meddw pob balch ar waddawd ei annoethineb.

870

Out of sight,
Forgotten quite !

Allan o olwg, allan o feddwl.

871

Those the most greedily inclined
Are those who leave the most behind.

Llawer o weddill o feddwl chwannawg.

872

Through all life's stages
The soul never ages.

Ni hena meddwl.

873

He, who never gave a thought,
Has to reconsider nought.

Ni feddwl, ni adfeddwl.

874

When for his cure a fool you're treating,
Begin and finish with a beating.

Meddyginiaeth ynfyd ffonawd dda.

875

The slightest courage will avail
To make the o'erbearing bully quail.

Gwan yw gormes gerbron y glewder lleiaf.

876

Oftenest and most,
Fail brag and boast.

Angwhanegid mefl mawrair.

877

Reproach be and dole
To the mouse of one hole.

Mefl i'r llygoden untwll.

878

If your beauty should smile,
You will kiss her the while.

Tra gweno meingan, cipia gusan.

879

Large ricks are made
Of sprout and blade.

Gnawd o egin meithrin das.

880

Wisdom, like the honey's sweetest,
Lowest lying still thou meetest.

Doethineb, mal goreuon y mel, a fydd yn isaf.

881

Hiccoughing children of their strength give token ;
An old man's hiccough speaks him faint and broken.

Ig ar blentyn cryfiant, ar henddyn methiant.

882

Bald head will never credit gain,
Unless his bald head show his brain.

Ni choelir y moel, oni welir ei emenydd.

883

The wise his rage
Will soon assuage.

Ni lydd doeth yn hir mewn llid.

884

A foe, and that a savage foe,
Is wind that from the east doth blow.

Gwynt o'r dwyrain, gelyn milain.

885

A kernel to take,
The stone you will break.

Rhaid tori y mesglyn cyn cael y cnewullyn.

886

The acorns, given for your own,
Surpass your honey upon loan.

Gwell messaig yn rhad no melsaig yn echwyn.

887

Which of the two were better said,
'There was he slain,' or, 'There I fled'?

Gwell 'mi giliais' nog 'efe a laddwyd.'

888

Sooner will storm the oak uproot,
Than 'twill the bramble at your foot.

Cynt y cwymp dar, no miaren, o flaen y gwynt.

889

He most possesses
Whom God blesses.

Nid meuedd ond asswyn Duw.

890

Little gain is smart attack,
Made but to be beaten back.

Ennill ' mi hw,' a cholli ' mi ha.'

891

A ram on his rambles
Gets a hatred of brambles.

Cas myharan mieri.

892

Of all God's creatures, made and seen
As good, the salmon was most clean.

Yr eawg glanaf un mil a luniwyd.

893

Of brutes, unhappiest brute is he
Whom eyes of owner never see.

Gwae mil, ni wyl ei berchen.

894

Seldom will slip belie its root :
The villain's father was a brute.

Gnawd mab taer yn filain.

895

Plashy and fat
Is the soil of the flat.

Gnawd merydd y' mro.

896

An infant maid, and greyhound pup,
Those ne'er enjoy who bring them up.

Ceneu milgi, a morwyn, ni cheiff eu mwyn, a' u maco.

897

The greatest feats of warriors true
Are those, that greatest mischief do.

Gorchestion milwyr drygu am y goreu.

898

The lazy makes a long delay,
E'er even a wrong he will repay.

Ni moch ddial mefl merydd.

899

If priest or monk on oath shall say
That he did see, by light of day,
The thing that hath been stol'n away
Within the culprit's hand, 'tis plain
By whom that stolen thing was ta'en.

Dognfynag cyfreithiawl yw llw crefyddwr, a dyngo weled y lleidr
liw dydd goleu a'r lledrad ganddo.—*Laws.*

900

A trifler he who sells his honey,
And then buys treacle with the money.

Gwerthu mel i brynu peth melyn.

901

If you escaped when at the pinch,
What matters it, by mile or inch?

Cystal modfedd a milltir o ddianc.

902

To make our manners, what they should be,
Laws might we let be, what they would be.

Moes, yna cyfraith.

903

Three things a Christian man desires :
What right decrees ;
What God shall please ;
What universal love inspires.

Tri moethineb cristion : darpar Duw ; a ellir gan a fo cyfiawn i
bawb ; ac a allo cariad at bawb ei arfer.

904

A good old age
Is virtue's wage.

A fo moesawl
A fydd oesawl.

905

On every fool if horns did grow,
A hornless head would be a show.

Pe bai cyrn ar ben pob ffol, fo geid arian yn dda am ddangaws
gwr moel.

906

To pick his food, and choose his cate,
The marten is most delicate.

Nid moethus ond bele.

907

What is nice,
Is asked for twice.

Melys moes eto.

908

What so glib is in its going,
As water to the eaves a-flowing ?

Mor hylithr a dwr hyd asbant.

909

Who thinks to speed, and takes no trouble,
Is making voyage on a bubble.

Gobaith heb gais,
Mordwy heb long.

910

The house, where stolen goods are found,
Is forfeited from roof to ground,
And all within it,—when withdrawn
The pledge is, which was left in pawn.

Y ty, y caffer lladrad ynddo, fydd halawg-dy, ac a fo ynddo, eithr adneu.—*Laws*.

911

In a child's conduct is but seen
What his bringing up has been.

Moes mab yn ol ei macer.

912

Who e'er can need his patience more,
Than dumb man at a deaf man's door?

Hir y bydd y mud y' mhorth y byddar.

913

If ' glutton ' cease to be a name,
' Cormorant ' will mean the same.

Nid glwth ond mulfran.

914

Twice and again will Humbug say,
' God's blessing on this house I pray.'

Teirgwaith y dywed mursen, ' Bendith Dduw yn y ty.'

915-6

That praise may seldom make us proud,
'Tis seldom till our death allow'd.

Balch pob moledig.
Moliant gwedi marw.

K

917

Cruel reminder kindly meant
To bedrid crone a distaff sent.

Mal cogel gwraig fusgrell.

918

No mine but of gold
For a mine should we hold.

Nid mwyn ond mwyn ariant.

919

Dire is the smoke's signification
In land without a population.

Arwydd drwg mwg yn niffaith.

920

Of mead it is the genial task,
From off the man to strip the mask.

Medd a ddiosg y mwgwd.

921

Though affectation female be,
Coxcombs in plenty you may see.

Mursen fydd o wr fal o wraig.

922

The beetle's single stroke will do
More than a hammer can with two.

Gwell un dyrnawd a'r ordd no dau a'r mwrthwyl.

923

All are assured,
When any is cured.

Lles pawb, pan feddyger.

924

The voice may be a blackbird's note,
The message suit a wolfish throat.

Genau mwyalch ac arch blaidd.

925

No mutilation
Like prostration.

Nid methiant ond musgrelli.

926

By gentle words new force is lent
To the strongest argument.

Gair mwyn a wna y ddadl yn gadarn.

927

By maiden alone
Is tenderness shown.

Nid mwynder ond merch.

928

Take full measure
Of the pleasure
All thy goods allow to thee ;
While the miser
Flays the devil
For less hide than holds a flea.

Cymer fwyniant y peth sy genyt, tra bo y cybydd yn blingaw y
diawl am lai no chroen chweinen.

929

Of kine three score and three he pays,
Who e'er a native noble slays ;
Nor less the penalty and pain,
If the king's foreign guest be slain.

Galanas boneddig cannwynawl ac alltud brenin tair buw, a
thriugain buw.—*Laws.*

K 2

930

Little and often take thy food ;
Little and seldom drink is good.

Bach a mynych fwyta ;
Bach ac anfynych ddiota.

931

Thou'lt need for every work of skill,
The tools, the talent, and the will.

Tri chyfraid pob gwaith : modd ; medryd ; a myn.

932

Little his life is better than a curse
Who a disgrace must in his bosom' nurse.

Gwae a fo a'i fefl yn ei fynwes.

933

If for your dog a larder you provide,
Whene'er you want him, take a look inside.

Atfai cell i gi,
Mynych ydd ai iddi.

934

Better at sea be helpless tost,
Than upon unknown mountains lost.

Gwell anghenawg mor
Nog anghenawg mynydd.

935–6

Rather be he that asks denied,
Than by thy promise not abide.

Gwell nag nog addaw ni wneir.

937

Give not thy old path away
For the path thou find'st to-day.

Na choll dy hen ffordd er dy fordd newydd.

938

To shave thy cheek,
Shave it sleek.

Naddiad dy foch nadd yn rhwy.

939

Fie on 'he,'
Who should be 'she.'

Och wyr, nad aethant yn wragedd.

940

By good men let thy love be had;
And bear no hatred to the bad.

Car y dyn da ; ac nag anghar y dyn drwg.

941

Two poisons by their venoms will
Each the other's venom kill.

Y naill wenwyn a ladd y llall.

942

When Make-believe shall woollen own,
On every peg will hang a gown.

Pan fydd gwlan gan fursen, y bydd gwn i bob cawnen.

943

Not all discern
A fox in fern.

Naill ai llwynog ai llwyn rhedyn.

944

Unless God's arm
Avert the harm,
Where mother slips,
There daughter trips.

Oni cheidw Duw rhag nam,
Fe dripia 'r ferch lle tripia 'r fam.

945

A ' but,' as big as man e'er spoke,
Will not a sturdy envoy choke.

Ni thag ' namyn ' cenad.

946

A wife's advice will seldom better make it ;
But woe betide the man who does not take it.

Bychan y tal cynghor gwraig ; ond gwae wr, nas cymero.

947

His is, of all, the poorest lot
Who makes poor use of what he's got.

Nid tylawd, ond nas cymero.

948

If once the wolf a mirror pass,
He ne'er will love a looking-glass.

Ni nawd gymmydd blaidd â drych.

949

The strongest fence
Is innocence.

Goreu nawdd diniweidrwydd.

950

'Tis hard to foil
Ingenious toil.

Ni nawd difenwir cywraint.

951

Nine nights with darkness you may veil,
And yet nine months will tell the tale.

Cyd celer nawnos,
Ni chelir nawmis.

952

Better one 'nay'
Than twice a 'yea.'

Gwell nag no dau eddewid.

953

A messenger that is belated
Brings you a message to be hated.

Cenad hwyr drwg ei neges.

954

If February's gale outbreak,
Forth from the nest it blows the snake.

Chwefrawr chwyth
Neidr o'i nyth.

955

To this owes mischief half its force,
That it has weakness for its source.

Ei nerth yw annerth diriad.

956

A bard hath privileges three :
Food, everywhere, and lodging free ;
Weapons are in his presence sheathed ;
Against his word no word is breathed.

Tair braint beirdd Ynys Prydain : trwyddedogaeth lle yr elont ;
nas dycer arf noeth yn eu herbyn ; a gair eu gair hwy ar bawb.

Bardic.

957

The grass, where nearest to the ground,
Sweeter than all the rest is found.

Melysaf y gwelt nesaf i'r ddaiar.

958

Rare skin, that, in its gloss and dye,
Can with the chequer'd adder vie.

Cyfrithed a neidr.

959

Perfect shelter, ne'er so small,
Is as good as spacious hall.

Neuadd pob diddos.

960

Not pleasure, but gain,
Is a change of our pain.

Newid y gwewyr.

961

Your surfeit of an hour is dear,
If you starve for it a year.

Gloddest awr a newyn blwyddyn.

962

Who cannot servants' faults forgive,
As servant to himself should live.

A'r ni oddefo gwas, bid was iddo ei hun.

963

No mother's child will ever bear
His famished mother's fast to share.
Nor famish'd mother e'er permit
Her children to be hunger-bit.

Ni ddwg newyn mam weision.

964

Strife badly will end,
When with God you contend.

A Duw nid da ymdaraw.

965

No scandalmonger drives his trade
In that, which of himself is made.

Enllib ni char ei enllibio.

966

All the wisdom you gain
You will pay for in pain.

Ni cheiff bwyll, nis pryno.

967

The wise, when he would swim a stream,
To breast the current does not dream.

Ni nofia mewn un afon
Y doeth yn erbyn y don.

968

Let triflers await
The grasshopper's fate :
For he all summer spends in song,
To famish all the winter long.

Mal ceiliawg y rhedyn, yn canu yr haf, a newynu y gauaf.

969

Whom we care for,
We forbear for.

Gwr, ni'th gar, ni'th gydfydd.

970

Of that has no man been deprived,
Which into being ne'er arrived.

Ni chyll niw dyfydd.

971

Autumn mists will wet your feet ;
Mists of winter fall in hail ;
Summer mists dissolve to heat ;
Mists at spring-tide brew a gale.

Niwl y gwanwyn gwasarn gwynt.
Niwl yr haf gwasarn tes.
Niwl y cynhauaf gwasarn gwlaw.
Niwl y gauaf gwasarn eira.

972

A child half clad will pass a merry day :
A child half fed is never seen to play.

Hwareuid mab noeth ;
Ni hwery mab newynawg.

973

Best brother to you
Is your guinea, if true.

Gwell ceiniog no brawd.

974

Assurance hath he doubly sure,
Who by his God is kept secure.

A noddo Duw, rhy nodder.

975

The creature that one hound hath taken
Will soon by all the pack be shaken.

Nugiaw gan y cwn.

976

Think not thy case from danger free
Whene'er a lord,
With naked sword,
Shall feel himself at home with thee.

Carueiddwch arglwydd a chledd noeth ys enbyd.

977

If once intemperance were slain,
No doctor could alive remain.

Lladd gloddest yw newynu y meddyg.

978-9

'Tis night that teems
The plotters' schemes ;
And day reveals
What night conceals.

Nos yw mam y cysylfäau.
Gwaith y nos y dydd a'i dengys.

980

The naked, one day, lend I loan,
The next, I get not back my own.

Dod fenthyg i noeth,
Nis cai dranoeth.

981

Genius is the combination
Of knowledge, mind, and inspiration

Tri bonedd awen : nwyf ; pwyll ; a gwybodaeth.

982-3

If long we pine
We breath resign ;
And better death
Than pining breath.

Hir nych i angeu.
Gwell marw no hir nychdawd.

984

Once at top,
There we'd stop.

O chyrhaedd fry
Ni ddaw obry.

985

While youth doth last,
The memory's fast.

Cof gan octid ys dir.

986

When yearning pain thy bosom heaves,
The utterance of a groan relieves.

Rhag trymfryd ochid achenawg.

987

Men hear with wonder, or a smile,
Of men in whom there is no guile.

Odidawg a fo didwyll.

988

The milk of dog, of cat, and mare,
The law's protection do not share.

Tri oferlaeth y sydd : llaeth cath ; llaeth gast ; a llaeth caseg ; can
ni ddiwygir dim am danaddynt.—*Laws.*

989

Bad luck to him who likes, the best,
Those hours when fowls are up at rest.

Noswyl iâr,
Gwae a'i car.

990

A May, that's bleak with frosty storm,
Your barn with what it holds will warm.

Mai oer a wna ysgubawr gynhes.

991

A claim will hold,
Though it be old.

Ni hena hawl er ei hoedi.

992

To back unclad, and empty maw,
Rarely will honour be a law.

Odid a gatwo wyneb o eisiwed.

993

To love a woman, spite of scorn,
Is to lick honey from a thorn.

Mal llyfu mel oddiar ddrain.

994

Have God's love still,
And fear no ill.

Cais Dduw yn gar,
Ac nag ofna far.

995

Carrion soon goes
Where the neighbours are crows.

Hir nis pery yr abwy, lle bo llawer o frain.

996

Faults of the honour'd honour win ;
The sins of teachers teach to sin.

Pechodau athrawon ynt athrawon pechodau.

997

If you make a lamb-like show,
Down a wolf's throat you will go.

A wnelo ei hun yn oen, a lyncir gan y blaidd.

998

To the man be no shame,
When his fortune's to blame.

Nid oes cywilydd rhag gofid.

999

'Tis promise rare,
If fruit it bear.

Odid addewid, a ddel.

1000

Well ground was the corn,
Where the mill is outworn.

Ys da felin, a ballodd.

1001

Larger the share that's wrung from fear,
Than love bestows on him that 's dear.

Gwell rhan ofn na rhan cariad.

1002

He will his youth the latest hold
Who earliest treats himself as old.

A fyno barau yn hir yn ieuanc, aed yn ebrwydd yn hen.

1003

Well thou starvest
Sloth in harvest.

Gwae oferwr yn nghynauaf.

1004

Strength let him gain,
Who would honour attain.

A tyno barch, bid gadarn.

1005

A watery bed with icy roof
Fish find not to be weatherproof.

Oer gwely pysgod yn nghysgawd iaen.

1006

For three, when trial they abide,
The king shall advocate provide :
      A woman lorn ;
      An alien born ;
A man whose voice would bring him scorn.

Tri dyn a ddyly tafodiawg yn llys drostynt gan y brenin : gwraig ;
ac alltud anghyfreithus ; a chryg anianawl.—*Laws.*

1007

The fox long jumped in vain pursuit
At hips ; then saw, they were not fruit.

Mal y llwynog am yr ogfaen.

1008

While harrow you're using,
Your quern will be bruising.

Tra rheto yr og, rheted y freuan.

1009

He who good is while long neglected,
Grows better still when he's respected.

Gwell gwr o'i berchi.

1010

Neither the tyrant, nor his minion,
Can rob the least of his opinion.

Rhydd barn i bawb.

1011

Would you the world's doings know,
Across your threshold you must go.

Ni cheiff chwedl, nid el o'i dy.

1012

Bad indeed must be the stake
That a year will rot and break.

Drwg pawl, ni safo flwyddyn.

1013

Men we druids falsely call :
True Druid is the God of all.

Nid derwydd eithr o enwawd ; nid derwydd ond Duw.

1014

Any child will overbear,
If his father's coat he wear.

Pawb a drais yn mhais ei dad.

1015

Less regardful is our mind
Of the great than of the kind.

Mwy parch hynaws no hynod.

1016

How unto mere
Clamour give ear?

Abandid ba andaw.

1017

Nothing that is bright and fair
With the peacock can compare.

Nid teg ond paen.

1018

Evil more rarely is undone,
Than two evils made of one.

Gwneuthur deuddrwg o'r un.

1019

Pots and pans are useful friends
Only, if a mind attends.

Pwyll a ddyly padell.

1020

As a mouse to the cat's paw,
A petty rogue is to the law.

Mal y llygoden dan balf y gath.

1021

Water will flow
To the valley below.

I'r pant y rhed y dwr.

1022

Good will never more be had
From a bad man, known for bad.

Drwg pawb o'i wybod.

1023

Reject the best that's at your call,
And you reject the best of all.

Goreu oll y goreu a ellir.

1024

'If with your thumb a coat you'll weave,'
Such are the 'ifs' which fools deceive.

Pe a bawd y gweid gwe.

1025

Beg not of nobles by a hint ;
Nor in a court your craving stint.

Ni rhaid pedi yn llys arglwydd.

L

1026

A horse is often seen to fall,
Though horse's hoofs are four in all.

Syrthid march oddiar ei bedwarcarn.

1027

As steel to the pole,
To duty is soul.

Mal y dur at y pegwn.

1028

Three cures for evil, while we draw our breath
On earth below,
Did God bestow.
The thought of fate ; oblivion ; and death.

Tri pheiriant Duw yn abred, er gorfod drwg, a chythraul, a dianc
oddiwrthynt at wynfyd : angen ; anghof ; ac angeu.—*Bardic.*

1029

Lifesome must that be, and spry,
Which can with the titmouse vie.

Mor binc a'r pela.

1030

Sayings that through the country rule
Are words too true for ridicule.

Hwedlau pen gwlad, rhy wir i hwerthin am eu pennau.

1031

Sins greatest are they
Done out of our way.

Drwg pechawd o'i bell erlid.

1032

'Mine,' says the canny, as the land he eyes ;
'I owned it once,' the simpleton replies.

Call, 'mi biau ;' anghall, 'bum berchen.'

1033

Of purest gold was made the tongue
Which in a wise man's head is hung.

Tafawd aur y' mhen dedwydd.

1034

Only when your arm you twist
Is elbow further off than wrist.

Nes penelin nog arddwrn.

1035

The safest place of self-defence
In peril is safe distance thence.

Goreu amddiffynfa digawn pell.

1036

The rule of a wife,
A daughter's ill life,
A son that is an untaught clown,
May turn the whole world upside down.

Pendodaeth gwraig ; digywilydd-dra merch ; ac anwybodaeth mab,
   a droant y byd wyneb i waered.

1037

Strong the judgment is and fast,
Which the ignorant has pass'd.

Pengadarn barn pob diwybod.

1038

Two-thirds of every great man's fame
Pack'd in a headpiece to him came.

Deuparth clod yn mhenglog.

1039

A tit at roast makes better fare
Than does a wild duck in the air.

Gwell penloyn yn llaw no hwyad yn awyr.

1040

Your chum is nearer to your heart
Than he with whom you sing a part.

Gwell car cell no char pennill.

1041

Heedless of his appointed day
Is he who heeds it far away.

Diawg i oed pwyllawg pell.

1042

Pretty everything that's small,
Except a devil's imp, we call.

Pert pob peth bach ond diawl bach.

1043

Into trouble if got,
An old woman will trot.

Angen a bair i henwrach duthiaw.

1044

Bold thief, who pawns a silver bowl
To him from whom his plate he stole.

Adneu gan berchen.

1045

No one need the world apprise
Whereabout the carrion lies.

Abwy a bair wybod lle bo.

1046

Out your game you'll never push
While you beat about the bush.

Troi o bobtu y berth.

1047

Maladies are great and small ;
But a peril lurks in all.

Yn mhob clwyf mae perygl.

1048

No clinging pain
Can you sustain,
But will end off
In a dry cough.

Peswch sych
Diwedd pob nych.

1049

For everything a time you'll find,
If its proper time you mind.

Amser sydd i bob peth.

1050

But short must be that noble's pedigree
Who hath not thief nor strumpet in the tree.

Byr ach bonedd, lle nis perthyn iddi na chrog na charn buten.

1051

When fortune daily favours sent you,
'Twas hourly mischief that she meant you.

Ffawd beunydd ys anffawd beuawr.

1052

If a madman bite, and slay,
No penalty his kin shall pay ;
Because disease it was, in truth,
Which murd'rous made the madman's tooth.

Os dyn cynddeiriawg a frath ddyn arall a 'i ddannedd, a' i farw
o'r brath, nis diwyg cenedl yr ynfyd, canys o anwyd yr haint
y colles efe ei fywyd.—*Laws.*

1053

Of little faith can be possest
He who is daily in its quest.

Bach yw crefydd, a chwilia beunydd am dano.

1054

On every side to touch, yet never handle
Your business, treats it like the moth a candle.

Peutu ac o beutu, fal y gwyf am y ganwyll.

1055–6

Of birds, that e'er on bush you spy,
Smartest and pertest is the pie.

Nid syw ond y bi.
Mor ffraeth a'r pia brith ar y berth.

1057

Sickening to death
Is a piper's breath.

Digu pawb o anadl y pibydd.

1058

The old cow's owner should not fail
To take his station at her tail.[1]

Pieufo y fuwch aed yn ei llosgwrn.

1059

The butterfly his coat displays,
The bee means honey, all his days.

Pilai yn ei wisg, gwenynen yn ei mel.

---

[1] Old cows rise with difficulty from the ground, and are helped by a lift at the tail.

1060

While your belly you pack,
You are stripping your back.

Y bol a bil y cefn.

1061

Time well good action,
Or you spoil it,
And break your egg
Before you boil it.

Piliaw wy cyn ei bobi.

1062

In restlessness, whate'er outsped
That bunting with the yellow head?

Mor binc a'r peneurin.

1063

Impolitic 'twas never found
To ring a pig which routs the ground.

Da trwyllaw trwyn mochyn a fo yn tiriaw.

1064

The quick by ready wit repair
The faults they make through want of care.

Rhaid wrth ammhwyll pwyll parawd.

1065

Proverbs that outlive their youth
Are the offspring of the truth.

Plant gwirionedd yw hen ddiarhebion.

1066

Many is the goose I know
Who no feathers has to show.

Mae llawer gwydd heblaw yr un, sy'n gwisgaw plu.

1067

The rod which to the stroke can ply
Beats that which into two will fly.

Gwell y wialen, a blyco, nog a doro.

1068

No meal 'twill take
No bread to bake.

Anhawdd pobi heb flawd.

1069

Gentle the sway
Which many obey.

Gweithred llary llywiaw nifer.

1070

Rich is one
Who oweth none.

Cyfoethawg pob diddyled.

1071

Things greatest of all
In beginning are small.

Bach yw pob peth yn ei ddechreu.

1072

Quickly will into bridge extend
That which now is but a bridge end.

A fo pen, bid pont.

1073

Bare is the plain
Which a sheep will disdain.

Llwm tir, ni phoro dafad.

1074

Rely not for thy life's sole stay
On that which men will throw away.

Nac ymddiried am dy borthwy i'r peth, a fwrir ymmaith.

1075

To be slender and tall,
Is still to be small.

Bychodedd
Meinoledd.

1076

He who will not feed his cats,
Must take kindly to the rats.

A'r ni phortho ei gath, porthed ei lygod.

1077

It does not need a skilful drover
To turn a bullock into clover.

Tryw i ych bori meillion.

1078

A pudding you waste
If a pudding you taste.

O'i mynych brofi bwytäwyd y boten i gyd.

1079–80

Of no man is a good word said
For which he has not something paid :
But, with this, in remembrance keep
That you may buy a good word cheap.

Ni cheir geirda heb brid.
Nid prid pryn gair teg.

1081

A woman upon trial taken
Will wait for marriage, till forsaken.

Y ferch a ddel i 'w phrofi
Hwyr y daw i'w phriodi.

1082

If into a barn she stray,
Your hen makes but one meal a day.

Un pryd yr iar yn ysgybawr.

1083

Whom in the land
None understand,
Misunderstanding all,
That man is he,
It needs must be,
Whom foreigner we call.

Anghyfiaith yw dyn, na wyper pa ddyweto, ac na wypo pa ddyweter
wrtho.—*Laws*.

1084

Who thinks not, nor by trial knows,
Without one anxious scruple goes.

Ni wyr pryder, nis prydero ac nis pryno.

1085

Better the beast whose price you take
Than that for which a price you stake.

Gwell eidion gwerth nog un pryn.

1086

Get plenty of care,
And sleep you will spare.

Dihunid a brydero.

1087

Good cheer hath fear of no denial,
But that refusing it a trial.
Nid erchis bwyd ond ei brofi.

1088

For woman's love, 'tis not the face
Most faultless that will win the race.
Nid wrth bryd cerid gwagedd.

1089

Better an ounce of wisdom bought
Than pounds of that which we were taught.
Gwell un synwyr pryn no dau synwyr parawd.

1090

A fig for him who by his pains,
In buying all, on nothing gains.
Cas dyn a bryno bob peth, ac heb ennill ar ddim.

1091

Your knowledge all you well may part with,
If it will buy you sense to start with.
Gwerth dy wybodaeth i brynu synwyr.

1092-3

Imprudence hath
A dangerous path,
Where no ills meet
The man discreet.
A fo da ei bwyll, a fydd diboen.
Ar nid yw pwyll, pyd yw.

1094

Regard a man, whoe'er he be,
If he have shown regard for thee.

Parch a 'th barcho pwy bynna bo.

1095

Three things will help you to your joint :
A knife that's keen ;
A plate that's clean ;
A fork that has a perfect point.

Tri pheth hoffaidd i wr ar ei giniaw : cyllell awchus ; pwyned
flaenllem ; ac alawr glan.

1096

Well doth the man deserve his shiver,
Who by the bridge side took the river.

Myned trwy yr afon a phont ar bwys.

1097–8

'Tis peril double deeds to do ;
Simplicity is peril too.

Ni bo awn pyd yw,
Ar nid yw pwyll pyd yw.

1099

No property, that you can buy,
Will pay its rent like industry.

Nid rhent ond diwydrwydd

1100

Those who a just complaint provoke,
Complaint by feign'd complaint will choke.

Achwyn rhag achwyn rhagddo.

1101

No easy task they undertake,
Who spite would into kindness make.

Nid hawdd rhadloni cenfigen.

1102

From taking a bad farm he shrinks
Who ne'er of a bad landlord thinks.

Ffo rhag drygdir, a'r na ffo rhag drwg arglwydd.

1103

Ere egg is laid,
Let nest be made.

Rhagnythed iar cyn dodwy.

1104

Happy it is for man that he
So little can before him see.

Da nad pell rhagwel dyn.

1105

Mostly in gloom
Do tempests loom.

Ucher a ddaw gan ddryc-hin.

1106

If all could have their wish when strong,
No soul on earth would ever long.

Pe caffai pawb a fynai,
Ni byddai hiraethawg neb rhai.

1107

A fool need never bear a bell
Where a fool is, the world to tell.

Ni raid dodi cloch am fwnwgl yr ynfyd.

1108

By the smallest share abides
He who into shares divides.

Lleiaf rhan rhan rhannwr.

1109

If the knife's handle well be made,
For granted you may take the blade.

Ys dir lladd y llafn wrth refed y troed.

1110

Not on the run
Is ploughing done.

Nid ar redeg y mae aredig.

1111

A blab as sure will silence break
As in a furrow will the crake.

Ni thaw mwy no rhegen yn y rhych.

1112

Better roam the mountains through,
And for bread the fern-root chew,
Than submit myself to you.

Byddai gwell genyf fyw ar y mynydd, a bwyta gwraidd rhedyn,
nog ymostwng iddynt.

1113

The curse that comes to good desert
Will never with it bring a hurt.

Nid adwyth rheg ni haedder.

1114

Folly soon will spoil the lot,
However good, which it hath got.

Drycai pob ammhwyll ei ran.

1115

He profit shuns
Who cuts and runs.

Nid a red a geiff y budd.

1116

Surpassing merit think to see
Yoked to some eccentricity.

Gnawd rhemp lle bo camp.

1117

To beg what otherwise you'll get,
Is to fish before your net.

Pysgota yn mlaen y rhwyd.

1118

Fire soon takes a hold
On a hearth that is old.

Hawdd cynneu tan yn hen aelwyd.

1119

Let those who wood and field deny,[1]
By fifty oaths prove alibi.
Not one, if life and limb 'twould save,
The oath of alien, or of slave ;
And three of fifty deeply sworn,
On horseback never to be borne,
To linen never comfort owe,
And never woman's solace know.

Y neb, a ddiwato goed a maes, rhodded lw deng wyr a deugain,
heb gaeth, a heb alltud ; a thri o honynt yn ddiofrydawg o far-
chogaeth, lliain, a gwraig.

[1] To deny wood and field means to plead absence from the scene and at
the time of some criminal act

1120

Ice its icy nature loses ;
Human nature change refuses.

Haws direwi rhew no dirywo rhyw.

1121

The want he has before his eyes
Will ne'er be suffer'd by the wise.

Angen, a ragwelir, ni ddaw byth ar ddoeth.

1122

A habit got will grow with thee,
Like the bark about a tree.

Mal y rhisg am y pren.

1123

Better in the dark to tramp
Than where the devil holds you lamp.

Nid da rhodio yn y gwawl,
Lle dalo diawl y ganwyll.

1124

When does love play,
Bucks waste away.

Pan fo addoed ar y geifr, y bychod a ridiir.

1125

Examine not the horse's eye
Which with your thanks alone you buy.

Ni edrychir yn lygad march rhodd.

1126

You'll claim but little to your good
A tree within another's wood.

Pren yn nghoed arall biau.

1127

Fire has no equal in destruction,
No rival water in obstruction.

Nid trais ond tan,
Nid rhwystr ond dwfr.

1128

The secret of two
Is their pledge to be true ;
If to three it be known
It is all the world's own.

Rhin deuddyn cyfrin yw :
Rhin tridyn cannyn a'i clyw.

1129

Your counsel is not worth a band
Cut from a fleaskin when it 's tann'd.

Ni rown ni garai o groen chwannen am dy gynghor.

1130

Let one, who loves to keep his whim,
Love those who beat it out of him.

A hoffo ei rosb,
Hoffed a'i cosb.

1131

Thickest blood-spots stain the crest
Which towers in battle loftiest.

Helm-gribawg rhuddfâawg fydd.

1132

For your soul it is ill,
Your body to fill.

Nid iachach yr enaid er llenwi y rhumen.

M

1133

Nature 'twas, that made the wont
Of a hog to grunt and grunt.

Rhyw i hwch ei rhwch.

1134

All ways a thoroughfare present,
But where there is entanglement.

Rhwydd, ni bo dyrys.

1135

If a doe in bounds you'd keep,
You must bar her of her leap.

Ni welais i lam rhwydd i ewig.

1136

No good thing on earth is such
But of it may be too much.

Nid da rhy o ddim.

1137-38

One word of warning will the wise,
A thousand will not dolts, apprise

Rhybudd i ddedwydd.
Rhybuddiaw trwch ni weryd.

1139

Did you try the ford and sound it,
Dare to praise it as you found it.

Moled pawb y rhyd, fal y caffo.

1140

Burnished be thy beads with praying ;
Rust thy sword through lack of slaying.

Bid lyfn dy baderau ;
Bid rydlyd dy arfau.

1141

A man whose chin a beard doth mask,
Only what he can get will ask.

Rhybrynawdd barfawg a eirch.

1142

With lengthened arm we reach in vain,
If the heart long not to attain.

Nid estyn llaw, ni rybuch calon.

1143

When priests have once begun to ban,
There lies some curse on every man.

Lleas pawb, pan rydyngir.

1144

Three forms to living things are given :
Dim rudiment within the deeps ;
The human shape which freedom keeps ;
Love and felicity in heaven.

Tri chyflwr hanfod bywedigion : cyflwr abred yn annwn ; cyflwr
rhyddid yn nyndawd ; a chyflwr cariad sef gwynfyd yn y nef.—
Bardic.

1145

He does not keep his secret well,
Who hides it in a parable.

Gochel ddammegu dy rin.

1146

The powerful spare
Their pains to beware.

Ni bydd cyfoethawg rhygall.

1147

Content with least respect be he
Who most familiar would be.

Ni bydd rhybarch rhagynefin.

M 2

1148

At a high price the man doth buy,
Who gets by importunity.

Rhybrynwys, a ryerchis.

1149

Good things, which to the wicked fall,
Will ever in enjoyment pall.

Ffawd i ddiriaid ni ryfain.

1150

Give the wonderful its day,
And the wonder fades away.

Rhewydd pob rhyfeddawd.

1151

He was betray'd while he was bred,
Who with pride-pampering food was fed.

Twyllid rhyfegid ryfygaid.

1152

In all things there may be excess,
Save in our penitent distress.

Nid da rhy o ddim.
Addwyn rhybenid i bechawd.

1153

Contention to breed
Is the devil's whole creed.

Golochwyd diawl annog rhyfel.

1154

He without spirit for the fight,
Who seeks not peace, is odious quite.

Cas a fo ryfelwr llesg, ac ni ddymuno heddwch o flaen rhyfel.

1155

Too much is often not one tittle
A better portion than too little.

Nid gwell gormodd no rhyfychan.

1156

If an idler win success,
His smallest winning is excess.

Ffawd i ddiawg nid rhyfaint.

1157

A rill you may dam
'Till a deluge you cram.

Hir argae a fag ryferthwy.

1158

One lov'd with love intense and true
As thoroughly was hated too.

Ni bu rygu na bai rygas.

1159

A trifler he, who wipes his share,
For the ploughing to prepare.

Sychu y swch i fyned i'r pridd.

1160

No misery that can befall
Is hidden long, and hidden all.

Ni rygelir dryglam.

1161

He who asks much on little claim
Goes back less lov'd than when he came,
Enrich'd in nothing but in blame.

Nid mawr i 'th gerid
Os rhwy a erchid.
Ni cheiff rhy anfoddawg.

1162

Daily your rye doth liker grow
The rye whose seed your hand did sow.

Po hynaf fo y rhyg tebycaf fydd i'w dad.

1163

A touch, and away,
Suffices for play.

Digawn yw gware rhynawd.

1164

Excessively small
Is the dearest of all.

Rhygu pob rhyfychawd.

1165

In difficulty pride we take ;
But ' Easy ' is the choice to make.

Gwell rhwydd no rhysedda.

1166

Of hogs the most still
Gets most of the swill.

Yr hwch, a dau, a fwyty 'r soeg.

1167

Better thy rising wrath compose
Than rush at once to deadly close.

Gwell dyhudd no rhysedda.

1168

He who a murder can commit,
The guiltless can accuse of it.

Sef, a ladd, a gyhudd.

1169

The fawn of a roe
Must gambolling go.

Rhyw i fab iwrch lammu.

1170

Of ten words heard
Take one for sooth,
And you may gain
A little truth.

Cred air o bob deg a glywi, a thi a gei rywfaint bach o wir.

1171

The dainty courtier, fenc'd with walls,
Only by love's arrow falls.

Gwnelid serch saeth syberw.

1172

You'll censure well the bowman's skill,
Before your own bow foeman kill.

Haws barnu no saethu.

1173

Thy mouth close up, and ope thine eye,
And heed unto thine ear apply.

Cau dy safn, ac agor dy glust a'th lygad.

1174

Saving is past
When you've come to the last.

Swylaw ar y cilyn diweddaf.

1175

Blindness warns, e'er it appears,
Year after year, for seven years.

Saith mlynedd y darogenir delli.

1176

Better a mastiff's temper know
Before you tread upon his toe.

Na sang ar droed ci chwerw.

1177

Of a serpent whole and hale
The strength lies ever in his tail.

Nerth sarph yn ei chloren.

1178

Knowledge earn
  While drawing breath ;
Not to learn
  Should hasten death.

Dysg hyd angeu, ac angeu i'r sawl, na ddysgo.

1179

Slaughter-houses you'll think sweet
When a soapmaker you meet.

Gwell dwylaw y cigydd no dwylaw y sebonydd.

1180

Better are means enough bestowing
Than are riches overflowing.

Gwell golud no rhysedd.

1181

Villany fails, and villains feel it,
Unless more villany conceal it.

Sef a lwydd i fefl ei chelu.

1182

The thing is rarely seen when eyed
That 's seen by the preoccupied.

Lygad y segur a wyl.

1183

The drunkards swill ;
  The idlers lag ;
But both help fill
  The hangman's bag.

Segurdawd a meddwdawd a wnant grogyddion yn gyfoethawg.

1184

Safe and silly is the war
Of the dog that bays the star.

Cyffoled a'r cwn yn cyfarth y ser.

1185

Stroke him on the side that's blind,
And the devil's self is kind.

Mae 'r diawl yn dda tra y sidaner.

1186

One who with hogs hath long been bred
Will like the grains on which they're fed.

A fegir gyda moch a ddysg fwyta soeg.

1187

When idlers leave their idle mood,
'Tis not for business that is good.

Ni moch wna da dyn segur.

1188

Dip not your hand into your bag
For every dog whose tail doth wag.

Agor ei law i bob ci, a siglo ei gynffon arno.

1189

Of all things eschew
The word that 's too true.

Rhygas pob rhywir.

1190

Nothing earthly hath a way,
Like a woman, to betray.

Nid siomedigaeth ond gwraig.

1191

Do thy sowing in the drought ;
Plant in streaming weather out.

Heu ar y sychin ; plannu ar y gwlypin.

1192

No marten cat with what is sweet,
No woman trust with sausage meat.

No bela i fel, no gwraig i selsig.

1193

Talk of the talk about your neighbour,
And talking is not worth its labour.

Son am y son amdano
Ni cheir son dda o hano.

1194

Better cheer
Is smallest beer,
   Quite thine own,
Than generous wine,
Thou callest thine
   Through gift or loan.

Gwell sucan meddiant no gwin cardawd.

1195

The thing to which we bear a hate
Is seen too soon, however late.

Rhygas rhywelir.

1196

Ill report about the strong
Into silence dies e'er long.

Ni saif gogan ar gadarn.

1197

Take no wife,
Have no strife.

Pwybynnag sy heb wraig, sy heb ymryson.

1198

Three things a hardy strength supply :
To lie on hair ;
To breathe cold air ;
To make our meal on food that's dry.

Tri pheth a gryffâant y corff : gorwedd ar wely caled ; wybren oer-
llyd ; a bwyd sych.

1199

He who hath habits of deceit,
Before he ends, himself will cheat.

Somgar a soma ei hunan yn y diwedd.

1200

Many a viper haunts the ground
Where the strawberries abound.

Lle aml y syfi, aml y nadredd.

1201

Better good sense
Than affluence.

Gwell synwyr no chyfoeth.

1202

Often laughing to excess
Is a trick of wantonness.

Gnawd gan rewydd rychwerthin.

1203

Nothing will pry
Like a covetous eye.

Nid sylwyn ond cybydd.

1204

Emblem of the undefiled
Is a primrose in the wild.

Mor ddiwair a symylen.

1205

The boy will little hurt receive,
Whose hand is on his father's sleeve.

Llaw mab yn llawes ei dad.

1206

Once your threshold overgone,
Half your journey will be done.

Cam dros y trothwy yw hanner y daith

1207

When teaching comes, the mother-wit
Is needed to make use of it.

Nid dysg heb synwyr.

1208

He who for nothing has to stay
Is already on his way.

A daclwys
A gerddwys.

1209

In a language unused
We are dumb or confused.

Gnawd syn syml anghyfiaith.

1210

You'll find no wife, whatever eyes you seek with,
So good as her who has no tongue to speak with.

Goreu gwraig gwraig heb dafawd.

1211

He mars his present in a trice,
Who gives a loaf, and asks a slice.

Rhoi y dorth, a gofyn y dafell.

1212

When the blind man throws his staff,
His tormentors win their laugh.

Mal dall yn taflu ei ffon.

1213

A clown will be clown,
Though wearing a crown.

Taiawg y bydd taiawg, cyd bo coronawg.

1214

If there's no joke in suffocation,
Poor is the fun of strangulation.

Brawd yw mygu i dagu.

1215

Better be carried by a jade
Than sprawling by an Arab laid.

Gwell march hagr, a'm dyco,
No march teg, a'm taflo.

1216

The strawberry had lost its way,
In the sow's stomach when it lay.

Syfien yn mola hwch.

1217

A torch brief light and wasteful lends
That hath a light at both its ends.

Tewyn a than y' mhob pen.

1218

For those who dance
The fiddlers play ;
Let those who dance
The fiddlers pay.

A gorelwo, taled i'r crythawr.

1219

That urchin's slice whom others hate
Will seem the nicest in the plate.

Hoff tam mab, ni charer.

1220

Death has not a care,
Whose forehead is fair.

Ni edrych angeu pwy decaf ei dalcen.

1221

One single morsel is the bread
With the butter on it spread.

Bara ac ymenyn un tamaid.

1222

For an hour thy tantrum stay ;
Thy tattle ever and a day.

Gochel y tampawg tros awr ; gochel y gwedwst tros fywyd.

1223

Talent which Sense does not command
Is but a torch in Folly's hand.

Awen heb ddoethineb tan yn llaw ffolineb.

1224

The leaf that rustles in the wind
With conscience thrills a guilty mind.

Llais dalen yn y gwynt a darf gydwybod euawg.

1225

The noise by perfect silence ne'er is mended,
Until the noisy silencing hath ended.

Goreu taw taw tewi.

1226

If to a man who is offending,
While thou art but thyself defending,
Thou dost the harm he was intending,
No lawful stay
Obstructs thy way.

O derfydd i ddyn wneuthur sarâad neu argywedd ar arall, pa
argywedd bynnag fo, os yn amddiffyn rhag y neb a argyweddir,
neu a saráer, os arddisgyn y weithred o'r cyffelyb fodd ar y ceisier
ei argyweddu yntau, ni ddyly y gyfraith ei luddiaw.—*Laws.*

1227

Quiet is the mischief brewing,
And silent is the mischief doing.

Boloch fydd daw.

1228

A moment's wrath the greyhound slew ;
For years the man his wrath did rue.

Tifaru fal y gwr, a laddwys ei filgi.

1229

Two, whose likeness makes a pair,
One another cannot bear.

Nid ef a byrth dyn ei debyg.

1230

Highest feat in wisdom's reach
Is the abstinence from speech.

Goreu o gampau doethineb tawedogrwydd.

1231

Youth may suppose ;
Age only knows.

Hen a wyr ;
Ieuanc a debyg.

1232

Let him whom a rude speech hath stirr'd
Take vengeance by a gentle word.

A ddialo air hagr rhoed ateb teg.

1233

Hateful is he who thinks he may
By overbearing get his way.

Cas a debyco orfod o falchder.

1234

'Tis the lucky man's roof
That is waterproof.

Adail dedwydd yn ddiddos.

1235

A child his toy, and all he knows
The empty, in a moment shows.

Anwybodus a ddengys yn fuan a wyr, fal plentyn yn dangaws
tegan.

1236

The wound our heedless youth did take,
In our old age begins to ache.

Hen y teimlir ergydion, a gaed yn ieuanc.

1237

Pride is but a way of brewing
For your fortunes a long ruin.

Gnawd wedi traha tranc hir.

1238

Three times shall wisdom be deceived,
For once that boldness is aggrieved.

Doeth a dwyllir deirgwaith ;
Ni thwyllir drud ond unwaith.

1239

Best share in the cake
Is the best we can take.

Goreu rhan o'r deisen un, a geffir.

1240

If hated quite, and worthless proved,
A man is by his sister loved.

Cerid chwaer diriad can ni charer.

1241

· Silent tongue and noiseless pace
Give the graceful half their grace.

Gnawd tawel yn delaid.

1242

The sun's bright face kills human sight ;
Look at his beauty in his light.

Edrych harddwch yr haul yn ei des, ac nid yn ei ffriw.

1243

One social home make sisters three :
Verse, scholarship, and history.

Brodyr teuluaeth : bardd; ysgolaig; a dadgeiniad.

1244

Object pitiful and vain
Is a king without his train.

Truan teyrn heb ei osgordd.

N

1245

'Twixt crown and eyes
Your fortune lies.

Ffawd pawb yn ei dàl.

1246

You to men must justice do,
For justice to be done to you.

Gwna iawn, ti a gei iawn amdano.

1247

The man whose mind no word reveals,
A world of wickedness conceals.

Tawedawg
Tew ei ddrwg.

1248

We cannot fly
Our destiny.

Ni eill dyn ochel tynged.

1249

That cause will be a cause indeed,
That doth not from a cause proceed.

Achos heb achos o hono.

1250

You'll see no jewel in your life
Like a jewel of a wife.

Goreu un tlws gwraig dda.

1251

A little courage will abate
The overbearing, which is great.

Gormes mawr a dawdd o flaen glewder bach.

1252

Debt melts not away
With the debtor's delay.

Ni thawdd dyled er ei haros.

1253

With skins the lawyer's roof is made
Of the litigious whom he flay'd.

Tai y cyfreithwyr a doir a chrwyn y cyfreithgar.

1254

No one asks the why and how
Of a tiff 'twixt dog and sow.

Mal y ci a'r hwch.

1255

What he swears,
No villain cares.

Ni ddawr diriad pa dyng.

1256

Handsome slices can we make
When we cut our neighbour's cake.

Hawdd toli yn helaeth o dorth gwr arall.

1257

Simpler than hiring
Is not requiring.

Haws toliaw no huriaw.

1258

Sworn brothers are, your lord protector,
The devil, and the tax collector.

Brodyr cyweithas arglwydd, tollwr, a chythraul.

1259

One friend you have sure
In your heap of manure

A gasglo domen, a gaiff un car cywir.

1260

The steer and ox are equal found,
Measur'd from belly to the ground.

Tyfid enderig o'i dòr.

1261

Rich is the storehouse which supplies
The unfortunate with miseries.

Mawr yw toraeth yr afwydd.

1262

Your tongue you may spare,
Your love to declare.

Nid rhaid tafawd i draethu serch.

1263

Although the river's wave be drink
Yet meat is not the river's brink.

Gellir yfed yr afon, ond nid ellir bwyta y dorlan.

1264

Hard is our case if dying be our will ;
And, dreading death, our case is harder still.

Mae yn dost ar a ddymunai farw ; mae yn dostach, ar a'i hofno.

1265

No aid we feeble can supply
Except we help to raise a cry.

Ni ddichon gwan ond gwaeddi.

1266

You'll praise the wise behind his back,
  If you would keep in his good graces :
But this need never make you slack
  To praise the women to their faces.

Canmawl doeth trach ei gefn ; a merch o flaen ei gwyneb.

1267

The honey then most freely flows
When through a sieve the honey goes.

Amlaf y mel tra hitler.

1268

For faint heart meet
Are nimble feet.

I galon wan
Da traed buan.

1269

Ask not the blind to undertake
The telling you when day shall break.

Gofyn i ddall a ydyw yn doriad gwawr.

1270

' Coming' of that you will not say,
Which is to come the following day.

Ni elwir daw hyd trannoeth.

1271

The stone rolls round
To level ground.

Treigl maen hyd wastad.

1272

Evil is a life of troubles :
Life without them evil doubles.

Drwg trallodau ;
Gwaeth hebddynt.

1273

A miser only then soft hearted
Is, when his groat and he have parted.

Edifar cybydd am draul.

1274

Great success has never hailed
Any man who never failed.

Ni llwyddodd,
Ond a dramgwyddodd.

1275

No meeting high is lawful there
Where fills the president his chair
While morning vapours throng the air :
But, if the noonday sunbeams smite
His empty chair, that day and night
No meeting high is held aright.

Amser i gadw gorsedd gyfreithlawn ydyw pan adnaper ei bod yn
bryd anterth : can ni ddylyir cynnal gorsedd y nos, na i dechreu
wedi hanner dydd.—*Laws.*

1276

As every sea must have a strand,
Beyond each ocean must be land.

Nid mor heb dramor.

1277 .

The sun of the west
Lights oxen to rest.

Trafferth ych hyd echwydd.

1278

To love is to be monarch quite ;
To dote is to be mad outright.

Nid breniniaeth ond serch :
Nid ynfydrwydd ond traserch.

1279

Cheap is the outlay of one penny
Which will save the cost of many.

Da traul ceiniawg, a weryd draul dwy.

1280

The stair whose steps are miseries,
Hath its summit in the skies.

Trallodion yw ffyn yr ysgol, sydd yn esgyn i'r nefoedd.

1281

Vainly by water they reside,
Who water at its further side.

Hol dwfr o draw i'r afon.

1282

Honour on man no place bestows :
The man takes honour where he goes.

Dyn a urdd y lle, ac nid urdd y lle y dyn.

1283

Purposes fail ;
Habits prevail.

Trech arfer nog arfaeth.

1284

Men find marriage near their homes,
Murder from a distance comes.

Dyweddi o wnc, galanas o bell.

1285

'Tis no great feat to make him cry,
Whose mouth already is awry.

Hawdd peri i fingam wylaw.

1286

Ere thou wrongest,
Be the strongest.

A fo trechaf treisied.

1287

Never yet has head been broken
For a word too kindly spoken.

Ni thyr pen er dywedid yn deg.

1288

The remorse begins to quicken
When the sin in years is stricken.

Tifeirwch newydd am hen bechawd.

1289

Birds of one hue
Flock to one view.

Adar o'r unlliw a dynant i'r unlle.

1290

An ill deed in a dingle done
Flames through the country like a sun.

Y fefl, a wneler yn rhin nant,
Hi a dywynyg y'ngwydd cant.

1291

The herd will often be astray,
To which a steer hath shown the way.

Mynych i'r praidd fod ar wall pan fo tywysawg yr enderig.

1292

What the weather to-day,
It is needless to say;
And it's wise to be dumb
About weather to come.

Am y tywydd goreu tewi.

1293

He who too high his climbing takes,
The topmost boughs beneath him breaks.

A ddringo yn rhy uchel, fe dyr y brigyn dano.

1294

For scattering one hand will do :
When you gather, take the two.

Bwrw a'th unllaw ; cais a'th ddwylaw.

1295

Storm, where it looms,
Sheds evening glooms.

Ucher a ddaw gan ddryghin.

1296

A dry cough is the warning sound
From a horn which Death has wound.

Udgorn a angau yw peswch sych.

1297

There is no fault within Hell's gate,
Except its want of setting straight.

Nid oes ar uffern ond eisieu ei threfnu.

1298

Pride and oppression
Shorten possession.

Traha a threisiaw gweinion a ddifa 'r etifeddion.

1299

When your success no bounds doth know,
Then faces you your deadliest foe.

Nid gelyn ond trallwyddiant.

1300

Twenty is beautiful :
Thirty is strong :
Forty will money make
All the day long
Fifty is wise with
Experience got :
The decades beyond it—
Oh, mention them not !

Ugaint teg ; deg ar ugaint cryf ; deugaint goludawg ; deg a deugaint
doeth ; a thros eu hoedrannau, nid gwiw son am y naill na'r llall.

1301

The fairer 'tis at morning light,
The fouler will it be ere night.

Po decaf y bore, hacraf yr ucher.

1302

As long as God is on His throne,
Well may he stand who stands alone.

Digawn Duw da i unig.

1303

Ever moving,
Unimproving.

Ni ddaw mad mynych dreigled.

1304

Our folly that we will not see
To-day, to-morrow felt shall be.

Na fynno weled ei ynfydrwydd heddyw, ef a'i teimla y fory.

1305

Truth is a spark,
That shines in the dark.

Llewychid gwir y' nhywyll.

1306

Maids their love will rarely give
In the village where they live.

Ni char morwyn mab o'i thref.

1307

The silliest imp that you can meet
Is the imp of self-conceit :
But in so black a skin doth dress
No imp in hell, as selfishness.

Y diawl ffolaf yn uffern yw hunandyb.
Hunanoldeb yw y diawl duaf yn uffern.

1308

Words utter well
What men would tell.
Deeds only show
What men would know.

Tafawd a draith :
Buchedd a ddengys.

1309

One hand the worse is
She, that nurses.

Unllawiawg fydd mammaeth.

1310

The bird that has been hatched in hell
Will in no other climate dwell.

Yr aderyn, a facer yn uffern, yn uffern y myn drigaw.

1311

Lost was the tooth not quite in vain,
That broke in gnawing through a chain.

Nid coll darfod o'r daint, a dreulied yn ysu y gadwyn.

1312

> A rolling stone
> No moss can own.

Maen, a dreigla,
Ni fysygla.

1313

> First praise thy neighbourhood as best,
> And in it then set up thy rest.

Canmawl dy fro,
A thrig yno.

1314

> Sneezes two
> No murder do ;
> Nor sneezes four
> Drive death from door.

Nid â untrew na dau i angeu.
Nac untrew na dau ni nawdd rhag angeu.

1315

> Of men there are three kinds : God's man
> Who good for ill gives, when he can :
> The man to this world's mind, who still
> Gives good for good, and ill for ill ;
> The devil's man, whose favourite way
> Is good with evil to repay.

Tri dyn y sydd : dyn i Dduw, a wna dda dros ddrwg ; dyn i ddyn
a wna dda dros dda, a drwg dros ddrwg ; a dyn i ddiawl, a
wna ddrwg dros dda.—*Bardic.*

1316

> Have but of one eye the enjoyment,
> For five score eyes you'll have employment.

Unllygeidiawg a ddyly cant.

1317

Better does the ablest man
Than the ablest woman can.

Gwell mared gwr nog un gwraig.

1318

The thing which only two should know
Will soon into a quarrel grow.

Rhin elid yn drin.

1319

The primal unities are three,
Which in the world must ever be :
One God ; one Truth ; one central Peace,
Where balanced oppositions cease.

Tri un cyntefig y sydd, ac nis gellir amgen nog un o honynt : un
Duw ; un gwirionedd ; ac un pwnc rhyddyd, sef y bydd lle bo
cydbwys pob gwrth.—*Bardic.*

1320

The eagle and mole
Keep not the same hole.

Nid untref gwadd ac eryr.

1321

He who an ill path takes one day,
Can find, the next, an evil way.

A fo drwg unwaith, a wyr fod yn ddrwg yr eilwaith.

1322

Stronger is the twisted twine
Than the twist of single line.

Cadarnach yw yr edaf yn gyfrodedd nog yn ungor.

1323

From this to that side
The nobleman wry'd
When up the ascent
To heaven he went.

O gam i gam, mal gwr boneddig yn rhodiaw y ffordd tua nef.

1324

Take not to Rome
The ways of home ;
Nor homeward bear
What ways are there.

Moes pob tud
Yn ei dud.

1325

On, on ! thou tired
Brute we've hired !

Tw ! farch benthyg.

1326

The concert proves a sorry jig,
That's made by nightingale and pig.

Nid ungerdd hwch ag eaws.

1327

My lady once to swim went down,
And then did of her swimming drown.

Unwaith, yr aeth yr arlwyddes i nofiaw, hi a foddes.

1328

If the wise slip, he soon will feel
The spurn of every blockhead's heel.

Pan lithro doeth, pob ffol a dery droed arno.

1329

Wholesomest of meats is bread :
  Of sauces milk is wholesomest :
A flowing brook, in gravel bed,
  Is of all beverages best :
The healthiest toil gives earth its fruit :
The healthiest pleasure is the lute.

Iachaf o fwyd bara : iachaf o enllyn llaeth : iachaf o ddiawd graian-
ddwr nant : iachaf gwaith trin y ddaiar : iachaf o lawenydd
cerdd dant.

1330

He who lays thorns upon the floor
Should not go barefoot past the door.

A heuo ddrain na cherdded yn droednoeth.

1331

Bold is the tone
Of one singing alone.

Hydr anaw unig.

1332

They who by reason wrong defend,
One fiend into two devils mend.

A ddadla dros ei fai a wna ddau ddiawl o un cythrawl.

1333

No place can less religion boast
Than where it is debated most.

Nid llai y crefydd yn unman no lle bo mwyaf y dadlu am dano.

1334

Though all things else will change and roam,
Truth ever truth is, and at home.

Gwir tios byth yn yr unman.

1335

An honest name two parts in three
Is of the highest dignity.

Deuparth urddas enw da.

1336

Never let your praise be lost
To the bridge by which you cross'd.

Canmoled pawb y bont, a'i dyco drawo.

1337

An old horse weens
If bran be beans.

Adwaen hen farch us.

1338

O'er the two highest shoulders will
There be a head that's higher still.

Uwch pen no dwy ysgwydd.

1339

In proud Intellect's despite
Fortune will assert her might.

Trech digwydd no deall.

1340

Whatever honey fortune brings,
The wise will use to sweeten things.

A fo aml ei fel, rhoed ar ei uwd.

1341

Say ' Fie !' to him, when he says ' Fie '
To everyone, yet knows not why.

Wfft i'r dyn, a wfftio bawb, heb wybod mwy am dano.

1342

A cow will ail
Without her tail.

Rhaid i'r fuwch wrth losgwrn.

1343

Human freedom vainly chooses
What necessity refuses.

Trech angen no dewis.

1344

On the first of these three things
If a woman's love is cast,
Speedily that liking brings
Love of the second, and the last :
Upon her looking-glass to pore ;
To see her husband leave his door :
And in her bed a paramour.

Tri pheth sydd ar wraig, a garo weled y cyntaf nis anghar y ddau
arall : wyneb ei hun mewn drych ; cefn ei gwr o bell ; a gor-
dderchwr yn ei gwely.

1345

Of a perfect love will some
Be lacking till the grandchild come.

Ni cherir yn llwyr,
Oni ddelo 'r wyr.

1346

The path unto God
Is where Magdalen trod.

Fford Llanfaglan ydd air i nef.

1347

There is nothing like a hare,
Tricks to play, with tricks to spare.

Nid ystrywgar ond ysgyfarnawg.

O

1348
To one 'little,' many such
Added make a ' little' much.

Ychydig yn aml a wna llawer.

1349
He fortune's favour needs to beg,
Who on a rail has left his egg.

Mal wy ar drosol.

1350
A dismal countenance awaits
Some evil message from the Fates.

Wyneb trist drwg a ery.

1351
The longer time the corn o'ergoes,
The liker other corn it grows.

Po hynaf yr yd, tebycaf fydd i'r byd.

1352
'Tis an excellence in sport,
To be seldom, and be short.

Goreu ar bob chware ychydigder.

1353
Grain for man is proper meat :
Flesh is food that dogs should eat.

Yd-fwyd i ddyn ; cig-fwyd i gwn.

1354
To lie and to boast
Are but one thing at most.

Bost a chelwydd, nid deubeth ydynt.

1355

Men thirst before they drink ; but thirst
Is after drinking at its worst.

Ar ol yfed syched sydd.

1356

Take thy broth ere waiting cool it ;
Use thy chance ere chance o'errule it.

Yf dy gawl cyn oero.

1357

Expect, although thou conquer here,
Thy garland in a higher sphere.

A orchfygo yma, a goronir fry.

1358

Experience schools
All careless fools :
The wise are taught
By taking thought.

Addysg ffol ei ymbrawf :
Addysg doeth ei ymbwyll.

1359

Self-preparation for distress
Is the next way to happiness.

Ymbarottöi y gyhwrdd adfyd ; yw y ffordd nesaf at hawddfyd.

1360

Gold and silver still supply
The food which feeds iniquity.

Ymborth anwiredd yw aur ac arian.

1361

Better the thankless task to stay,
Than longer labour throw away.

Gwell peidiaw nog ymddireidiaw.

1362

The man who bears
The victual basket,
And wants a meal,
Had best not ask it.

A ddyco y god ymborthed o honi.

1363

The trick of tricks possess you would
Had you the trick of being good.

Dichell ar bob dichell ymddichellu daioni.

1364

We're ne'er deceived by false pretence
As by our own self-confidence.

Gwaethaf twyll twyll ymddiried.

1365

He who away life rashly throws,
Upon the devil it bestows.

A fwrw ymaith ei fywyd yn ddiachaws, marw dros y diawl y mae.

1366

Foil'd in his scheme the man will be
Who waits for opportunity.

Meflir a ymddir hamdden.

1367

Pitiful he who still relies
Upon some windfall from the skies.

Cas a ymddirieto i rodd.

1368

Recompense slowest under heaven
Is that which is for conduct given.

Hwyra' tâl tâl ymddwyn.

1369

To three things never trust afford :
The fineness of a winter's day ;
The self-exertion of a lord ;
The health of one in life's decay.

Tri pheth nid ellir ymddiried iddynt : iechyd hen ; hindda y
gauaf ; a diwydrwydd arglwydd.

1370

In her own snare will foul deceit
Often entangle her own feet.

Dichell a ymddyrysa yn ei chroglath ei hunan.

1371

Milk, butter, and honey
Are sauces three
Which will give us our health
Or will let our health be.

Tri enllyn iechyd : mel ; ymenyn ; a llaeth.

1372

Few great men will you find in such
As given are to talking much.

Nid mynych gwr mawr ymeiriwr.

1373

You'll do your foe the worst despite,
By doing always what is right.

A fyno ddial yn drwm ar ei elyn, ymfuchedded yn lan.

1374

Two who two lovers' secrets share
Small love unto each other bear.

Nid ymgar y llateion.

1375

Beware to shake
Fruit trees that break.

Ymmod pren, ni ddeil i'w ymmodi.

1376

When thieves are loud accusing thieves,
The honest then his own retrieves.

Pan el lladron i ymgyhuddaw, y ceiff cywiriaid eu da.

1377

Better in compromise to fail
Than by a lawsuit to prevail.

Gwell cydunaw yn ddrwg nog ymgyfreithiaw yn dda.

1378

The highest bliss we then are knowing
When receiving and bestowing.

Goreu ar bob gwynfyd ymgymwynasu.

1379

Only in sinning man offends ;
A devil sins, and sin defends.

Rhyw i ddyn bechu, ond rhyw i ddiawl yn unig, ymgadarnâu yn
ei bechawd.

1380

So fat the wealthy has been fed
Upon the tears by wretches shed.

Mae y goludawg yn ymfrasâu ar ddagrau y tlodion.

1381

The snuggest chest will never hide
A man who takes to its outside.

Ymguddaw ar gefn y gist.

1382

When itching plagues,
He must be poor
Who has no nails
To scratch a cure.

Nid oes ganddo yr ewinedd i ymgrafu.

1383

Anger is as good a plight
As courage, for a valiant fight.

Nid gwaeth yr ymladd dig no glew.

1384

He to the sea will never take
Who cannot conversation make.

Nid â ar for, nid ymlefair.

1385

Better is one who guards, than two
That will your treasure's thief pursue.

Gwell un ceidwad no dau ymlyniad.

1386

On ! on ! bids fly the guilty mind,
When no pursuer is behind.

Euawg a ffy lle nas ymlidier.

1387

The swimmer thought :
'Let boats upset ;
'While others drown,
'I am but wet.'

Ni waeth ganddo pwy a foddo, os gall efe ymnofio.

1388

Misfortunes gallop to befall,
But in departing only crawl.

Anffawd a ddaw dan redeg, ac â ymaith dan ymlusgaw.

1389

Better, before doing, one
Word, than two when all is done.

Gwell un gair y'mlaen no dau yn ol.

1390

He who himself on hire would let,
By difficulties is beset.
And he who takes himself on hire
Has made a bargain to admire.

Nid esmwyth ymgyflogi.

1391

If of a fire your seat you make,
The odds are long that fire you take.

Nid eisteddir ar dan heb ymlosgi.

1392

The vile his honour will betray
To speed another honour's way.

Cas dyn, a ymroddo mewn anurddas er urddas i un arall.

1393

That which was on a dunghill bred,
Of dung will like to make its bed.

A fagwyd ar y domen, a gar ymoloi yn y dom.

1394-5

He who an ill deed
　To his neighbour has done,
Will take a good heed
　His neighbour to shun :
But, though he complete
This dexterous feat,
The justice of God it is harder to cheat.

A wnel drwg ymogeled.
A ymogelo rhag dyn ni ymogel rhag Duw.

1396

A treat, and earn'd by pleasant task,
'Tis on a mountain-top to bask.

Dewisbeth ymorheula pen mynydd.

1397

Cats grapple and claw
When love is their law.

Wrth ymrabin y mae y cathau yn ymgaru.

1398

The secret you wish none to know,
Let not beyond your thinking go.

A fynno, na wypo neb ei rin, ymrined â'i bwyll yn unig.

1399

When evil its appearance makes,
Some shape of good it surely takes.

Ymrith y drwg ar lun daioni.

1400

'Tis labour light
To keep from sight.

Gwaith ysgafn ymogelid.

1401

Better to offer your left cheek
Than for the right your vengeance wreak.

Gwell ymroddwr no dialwr.

1402

Nigh all their health the healthful gain
From labour's pleasurable pain.

Deuparth iechyd ymrwysiaw.

1403

There is one thing more than two
That in haste 'tis best to do :
To catch a flea when flea you feel ;
　　To cure contention
　　By prevention ;
And from a mad dog's path to steal.

Tri pheth sy goreu eu gwneyd ar frys : dal chwain ; troi o ffordd
ci cynddeiriawg ; a gochel ymryson.

1404

What good was in you at the first
To lose, of worst things is the worst.

Gwaeth no phob gwaethaf ymwaethu.

1405

Love one who does not love repay,
And thou hast thrown thy love away.

O cheri di, ni'th garo,
Collaist a geraist yno.

1406

Let your quarrel end before
Some foolish meddler make it more.

Gad ymaith ymryson cyn ymyryd arni.

1407

Happy for thee
Reformed to be
Not under terror's strong control,
But by thy reasonable soul.

Gwyn ei fyd, a ymwelläo o gynghor ei bwyll, ac nid o gynghor ei
ofnau.

1408

If at your door Misfortune stand,
She'll bring instruction in her hand.

Adfyd a ddaw
A dysg yn ei law.

1409

Better in hut your home to see,
Than homeless in a palace be.

Gwell bwth yn gartref no llys yn alldref.

1410

Simpletons fumble steel to find ;
A wise man's weapon is his mind.

Arf doeth pwyll, arf ynfyd dur.

1411

As into years a Welshman goes,
More foolish year by year he grows.

Po henaf y Cymro ynfytaf fydd.

1412

The learned ever love bestow
Upon the things of long ago.

Cerid doeth yr encilion.

1413

In the middle of the sea
More than fishes there must be.

Mwy no physg y' mysg mor.

1414-5

Three evils daily do decline
Under the stress of powers divine :
Ignorance ; and hatred strong ;
And the wont of doing wrong.
And three things daily might acquire,
By the love which they inspire
All within their sphere to draw :
Knowledge ; charity ; and law.

Tri pheth sydd yn ymwanâu beunydd gan faint pennaf yr ymgais yn eu gwrth : cas ; camwedd ; ac anwybodaeth. Tri pheth sydd yn ymgadarnâu beunydd, gan fod mwyaf yr ymgais atynt : cariad ; gwybodaeth ; a chyfiawnder.—*Bardic.*

1416

Odious is he, who none believes,
And who the trust of none receives.

Cas na chreto neb, na neb yntau.

1417

Best prisoner is a hog in sty :
Best neighbour, goat, that ranges by.

Goreu yngogiaid geifr :
Goreu amgyfyng moch.

1418

The dog that at all game will snatch,
No single kind of game can catch.

Y ci, a helio bob llwdn, ni bydd da ar yr un.

1419

Where'er hath strayed fair weather from your home,
Back with the north wind will the truant come.

Pan goller yr hinon, o'r gogledd daw eton.

1420

To all but the blind
Fools open their mind.

Ni chel ynfyd ei feddwl.

1421

No fool's worst fit of folly vies
With the love-madness of the wise.

Nid ynfydrwydd ond cariad.

1422

Of habits all none worse can be
Than from all habit to be free.

Arfer anarfer yw arfer waethaf yn y byd.

1423

If the way have long been clear,
Then the sticking-place is near.

Gnawd gwedy rhydeg yrthwch.

1424

Too often does reproach belong
To single life that has been long.

Mefl ys gnawd o weddwdawd hir.

1425

Each increase of a miser's store
But makes his misery the more.

Amledd cybydd ys tlodi arno.

1426

Poor wheat you'll breed
From thistle seed.

A he ysgall, ni fed wenith.

1427

Hunger will never
From idleness sever.

Nid ysgar newyn a diogi.

1428

Grass and thistles after rain,
And the alder, grow amain.

Tri pheth a gynnydd ar y gwlaw :
Gwlydd ; ac ysgall ; ac ysgaw.

1429

'Twas lightly sent ;
It lightly went.

Ysgafn y daeth,
Ysgafn yr aeth.

1430

Fair architecture gems the land
Where school and barn and stithy stand.

Tri harddwch gwlad : ysgubawr ; efail ; ac ysgol.

1431

See that a lion at your door
Be not a lion on your floor.

Ysgrubyl diriad yn eithaf.

1432

The laziest man can count the sheaves
The lazy from his field receives.

Hawdd rhifaw yr ysgubau ar faes gwr diawg.

1433

The wood-pigeon brings
Its strength in its wings.

Nerth ysguthan yn ei hadanedd.

1434

Your staff you push
Through many a bush,
Ere out you scare
A single hare.

Rhaid pwyaw llawer llwyn cyn cilio ysgyfarnawg.

1435

In the young 'tis inbred
To trot rashly ahead.

Rhyw i fab ysgyrchlamu.

1436

Each his share
Has of care.

Ys id ar bawb ei bryder.

1437

If a sore has long been such,
You can gall it by a touch.

Hawdd ysigaw hen glwyf.

1438

Disennobled by its place
On gown of hemp lies golden lace.

Ysnoden aur a gwn carth.

1439

No ravager is like the wind,
To take, and spoil what's left behind.

Nid yspail ond gwynt.

1440

Fire of the kiln will oft have hold,
While out and in the barn is cold.

Cynt y llysg yr odyn, no'r ysgubawr.

1441

The dress that's made no matter how
Sits like a saddle on a sow.

Gweddu, mal ystarn ar gefn hwch.

1442

Happy for a maid up-grown
If she's happy when alone.

Gwyn fyd y ferch, a allo fod gan ei hun.

1443

For ever fled
The word once said !

Nid adchwelawg gair.

1444

Those who lose digestive power
Lose their licence to devour.

Ni ddyly drwg foly namyn drwg ysu.

1445

The want of kind
A want we find.

Angen rhyw
Angen yw.

1446

'Tis farming ill, and not ill-hap,
That gives the fence so wide a gap

Adwyawg cae dryg-ammaeth.

1447-8

Of promise tall
The child is small ;
Yet promise smooth
A fool will soothe.

Addaw mawr a rhodd fechan.
Addaw teg a wna ynfyd yn llawen.

1449-50

Of good things given, that entrance make,
The porter may a handful take ;
And when a wain with billets full
Shall pass the gate, he one may pull
Big as his right hand can displace,
While the wain slackens not its pace.

Y porthawr a ddyly o bob anrheg, a ddel trwy y porth, ei ddyrnaid.
Y porthawr a ddyly bren o bob bennaid nid amgen pren a allo ei
dynnu a 'i un llaw heb lestair ar gerdded y meirch a'r ychain

Laws.

1451

In memory wisdom's seeds are rife,
Thought is the womb which gives them life.

Tad doethineb yw cof, a'i fam yw ystyriaeth.

1452

He who at venture draws his bow,
The random arrow must forego.

Y neb, a saetho ar adrybydd, a gyll ei saeth.

1453

A heart ill at ease
Brings a body disease.

Afiach pob trwmgalon.

1454

Pollution lingers
On lazy fingers.

Aflan dwylaw ddiawgswrth.

1455

Empty of food his stomach lies
Who children has of every size.

A fo aml ei feibion, bid wag ei goluddion.

P

1456

He washes best who swills the skin ;
Not he who soaks what is within.

Gwell gorne golchi nog un glythni.

1457

Half its due seed in earth you'll better drop
Than have but half a summer on the crop.

Gwell hanner had na hanner haf.

1458

The single desire
Of the cold is a fire.

Anwydog chwannog i dân.

1459

To be bounteous, bounteous mind
Something in the purse must find.

Nid ellir hael ar ni bo.

1460

Those to whom mischief has a zest
More love their mischief than their rest.

Diriad ni hawddfaidd heddwch.

1461

Three teachers wisdom will impart :
Suffering ; Thought ; and Truthful heart.

O dripheth y mae doethineb : gwirionedd, ystyr, a goddef.

1462

Modest and plain
Is history's vein.

Gŵyl yw hanes.

1463

More strength it needs
By force to wrest,
Than hold by force
What is possessed.

Trech à gais noe à geidu.

1464

Beauty is oft an ill to fear,
While very ugly's very dear.

Llawer teg drwg ei ddefnydd ;
Llawer hagr hygar fydd.

1465

Better that none should watch the kine,
Than he who on them hath design.

Arofyn drwg fugail.

1466

Till argument's ended,
Be judgment suspended :
And when judgment is past,
Let its word be the last.

Ar ddiwedd y mae barnu.

1467

Trust a wool dealer not to fail
In knowing where there's wool on sale.

Gwyr gwlanwr lle bo gwlan ar werth.

1468

One full of care his watch will keep ;
One full of sorrow falls asleep.

Ni chwsg gofalus, ac e gwsg galarus.

1469

Merry be she
Who nurse would be.

Afieithus pob mammaeth.

1470

No Irishman you'll get away,
Unless he lack the wit to stay.

Mal y Gwyddel am ei yru allan.

1471

Words forgot are ; words are broken ;
But can never be unspoken.

Nid a gair i adwedd.

1472

Nothing arduous hath such height
But labour will o'erget it quite.

Llafur a orfydd ar bob peth.

1473

No token you'd own,
If by all it were known.

Awgrym pawb ni's gwybydd.

1474

Faith in a false man's warrant placed
Is mortgage taken of a waste.

Arwaesaf à diffyd diffaith.

1475

If blood once flow upon the ground,
Though none complain, its lord is bound
To know the hand,
And whip the guilt,
Which on his land
That blood hath spilt.

Gwaed a reto hyd lawr, can ni chwyner amdano yr arglwydd a
ddyly ymyru wrth waedlydu ei dir.—*Laws.*

1476
You'll never school
A testy fool.
Anhydyn pob afrywiawg.

1477
No scruple e'er obstructs our way
The hundredth time we disobey
Gnawd as tyr gant orchymmyn.

1478
Of order little is he taught
Who collar buys for cow unbought
Aerwy cyn buwch.

1479
When the larder door stands wide,
You need not push your dog inside
Anaws ci i gell a gored.

1480
The heedless will
Be luckless still.
Anhapus pob trwch.

1481
The shaft of satire venom breeds
In bosoms conscious of ill deeds
Gogan sydd yn gorllymu cerydd a gwarth ar bob drwg

1482
He who is knowing in the laws
To law will take for little cause
A fo caled ynghyngaws,
Dadleued ar bob achaws.

1483

No bard is he
Who lacks these three :
A genius apt to make a verse ;
Lore that can mysteries rehearse ;
A life, than is the best, no worse.

Tri pheth nis gellir bardd hebddynt : awen wrth gerdd ; gwybod
cyfrinach barddas ; a chynneddfau da.—*Bardic.*

1484

What a child is taught on Sunday,
That a child will know on Monday.

A ddysger i fab ddydd Sul,
Ef a'i gwybydd ddydd Lun.

1485-6

To take, not having need to use,
Is waste, yet waste 'tis to refuse.

Afrad pob afraid.
Afrad yw gwrthod.

1487

He who to church the nearest lies,
Will furthest be from Paradise.

A fo nesaf i'r eglwys, fydd pellaf odiwrth baradwys.

1488

Fool more ridiculous was never
Than the fool who thinks he's clever.

Cas a dybio ei fod yn gall,
Ac yntau yn anghall.

1489

A little among neighbours to possess
Surpasses affluence in a wilderness.

Gwell bach yn nhrefred no mawr yn alldred.

1490

Avaricious and not mean
Is a monster never seen.

Anhael pob cybydd.

1491

Those who for small wrong raise a cry,
Therein a great wrong prophesy.

A gwyn cwyn bychan, cwyn mawr a ddarogan.

1492

Happy the privilege of some,
Who being worst the best become.

Myned ar y gwell o'r gwaeth.

1493

They soon forsake,
Who rashly take.

Anwadal pob ehud.

1494

Handsome ever is the sack
Whereinto we our winnings pack.

Braith ei god a gynnull.

1495

Set your dog on always so
That you with him do not go

Annog dy gi, ac na ddos ganddo.

1496

Of nothing possess'd
Ever distress'd.

Anghenawg
Pob tlawd.

1497

He who would stamp the cow-dung out,
But wider spreads the muck about.

Llettaf fydd y bisweilyn o'i sathru.

1498

Away to fling the iron ball ;
To tug and wrestle for a fall ;
And across hot coals to haul ;
Britons of old did pastime call.

Tri gwarau ymdrech oedd gan y Cymmry : gynt, gwarau ymsang ;
ac ymdaflu ag afalau dur ; ac ymdynnu ar draws tanau.

1499

' Silliman's ' tongue
Is lightly hung.

Annoeth llithrig ei dafawd.

1500

Evil was the hour and day
That put us in a scoundrel's way.

Awr ddrwg caffaeliad falswr.

1501

A curse, beside his loss of ease,
The horse will get who breaks his knees.

Bai ar farch dorri ei droed.

1502

The old, when famished, takes a bone,
Because 'tis tenderer than a stone.

Asgwrn yr hen
Yn yr angen.

1503

' Darling mine,' and ' sweetest dear,'
Lovers all will say and hear.

' Anwyl ' gan bawb, a gâr.

1504

On taste they pall
Whose sense is small.

Anghymmen pob ffol.

1505-6

Less easily you'll cheat the blind
Than the man who's weak in mind ;
And more than half of eyes bereft
Is he, whose right hand is a left.

Anghall mal dall a dwyllir.
Dall pob anghyfarwydd.

1507

Would you your neighbour love, be slack
To know his talk behind your back.

A garo ei gilydd nid adnebydd ei gabl.

1508

Disease and sleep
Apart will keep.

Nid cyd-dyun hun â haint.

1509

Freely let a rover roam,
To burn another rover's home.

Anrhaith gyfludwydd taiawg yn nhy ei gilydd.

1510

A primrose glistening in the shade
Is the wafer Nature made
On God's high altar to be laid.

Briallu teg afrllad hael.

1511

Of all things precious is and dear
His eye to one who seeth clear.

Golwg yn yd gwyl yd gâr.

1512

Our comfort is sold
So long as we're cold.

Anghynnes pob oer.

1513

Death speeds his way,
And keeps his day.

Angeu a ddyfrys.

1514

Something was scanted
Where anything's wanted.

Anghwbl pob eisieu.

1515

Town cats would all the better fare
If masters loved not country air.

Gwell i'r gath nad elid i hafotta.

1516

Those who terribly endure
Make of silence all their cure.

A oddef ry tau.

1517

He who falls, his foe defying,
Housel'd is by Fame in dying.

A fo marw er ei fygwth, a'i faw y cymmuner.

1518

Each man holds, by all opinion,
O'er his own a lord's dominion.

Arglwydd pawb ar eiddo.

1519

He gold is saving
Who gold is craving.

Aur gan bawb, a chwennych.

1520

The weapon is keen
That shaves you clean.

Awchus arf a eillio.

1521

For maker of the song you'll quote,
Not him who sang, but him who wrote.

Awdur cerdd, a'i gwnel.

1522

Under each roof, of tile or straw,
Its owner will lay down the law.

Athro pawb yn ei dy.

1523

High head and no feet
Pride's figure complete.

Balchder heb droed.

1524

Far and faint as is the cry
Of the puttock who flew by.

Pellach bellach fal chwedl y barcut.

1525

A heart that's quick to boil with rage
Is the lion's heritage.

Berwid calon llew.

1526

If hogs are blessed, be certain that
The man who blesses owns their fat.

Bendith i'r hwch biau 'r bloneg.

1527

Laugh at his rashness as you will,
' Foolhardy ' will be headlong still.

Bid ehud drud er chwerthin.

1528

While man in inchoation here
Is striving to a higher sphere,
For three sins must he backward fall,
Though loyal else to good in all :
If cruelty his fault shall be,
As great or small, so sinketh he ;
And if from truthfulness he swerves,
His lapse is still as that deserves ;
But if unseemly pride he shows,
Down to the lowest depth he goes.
And thence again the steep ascent
All travel up, as first they went.

O dri pheth y syrthir yn abred gan angeu er ymlynu yn mhob
peth arall wrth y da : o falchder hyd anwn ; o anwiredd hyd
obryn ; ac o anrhugaredd hyd gydfil a threiglo yn ol, at ddyn-
dawd fal o'r blaen.—*Bardic.*

1529

Perfect be the share in all
That but waits a wish's call.

Bid gyfa rhan a rybuchir.

1530

Mangled and cold the banquet lies
Which a massacre supplies.

Oer yw isgell yr alanas.

1531

Safe in the strife
Is a messenger's life.

Ni leddir cennad.

1532

Truth alone the lips can part,
When the truth is in the heart.

O gywirdeb y galon y dywed y genau.

1533

Neither hen it grieves, nor chick,
That the hawk has fallen sick.

Ni chwyn yr iar fod y gwalch yn glaf.

1534

No pleasure but in greenest grass
The dainty mare e'er found ;
And, reaching what did all surpass,
The dainty mare was drowned.

Yn ceisiaw y blewyn glas y boddes y gaseg.

1535

We perceive not how each day
Winter's sharpness wears away.

Lleilai lymaid gauaf.

1536

No man is boor
On Berwyn moor.

Nid iangwr neb ar Berwyn.

1537

Clever coaxing and caress
Win surly dogs from surliness.

Llofelwch gi chwerw.

1538

They, whose detraction brightens, own
The genius of a grinding stone.

Awen maen llifiannu.

1539

As heavily upon your crown
Will weigh your white hair as your brown.

Nid trymach y blewyn llwyd no'r gwyn.

1540

Nothing can you name again
That is wasteful as a hen.

Nid afradlawn ond iar.

1541

Who starves himself, he
But a starveling will be.

Bid wyw gwr heb fagwraeth.

1542

Never from your house should lie
The deed of lease you hold it by.

Rhag myned un llog o'r ty.

1543

In no vessel can you jam
More than will the vessel cram.

Ni eing mewn llestr ond ei lonaid.

1544

Never listen to the story
That an old head is not hoary.

Llwyd pob hen.

1545

If God your having do not please,
Having the best brings little ease.

Ni fynno Duw ni lwydd.

1546-7
Hearts never sink
Through health or drink.

Bid lawen yr iach.
Bid lawen y meddw.

1548
Be more his justice than his pity,
Who whips the mayor in his own city.

Cosbi y maer yn mhen y dref.

1549
Weed, thorn, and bramble soon will hide
The field that is not occupied.

Mae wedi myned yn abred gwyllt.

1550
Of a wicked man the steer
Will not be ox for many a year.

Hir y bydd enderig ych drygwr.

1551
No army can muster
Like bees in a cluster.

Byglymu fal gwenyn.

1552
Eight, men and maiden, slaves shall be
Deliberate slaughter's penalty.

Y neb a laddo ddyn o gynghorfyn taled bedwar gwas, a phedair
morwyn.—*Laws.*

1553
Paragon of creatures bland
Is a kid that's rear'd by hand.

Mal myn magawd

1554

Nor prayer nor strength can arrow bring,
Once parted, backward to the string.

Mal y saeth o'r llinyn.

1555

Gigantic be the work as fair
That would with Merlin's ' henge ' compare.

Mal gwaith Emrys.

1556

A grinding mill
Have water will.

Y felin, a fal, a fyn ddwfr.

1557

From one ill word, in malice said,
Often is deadly mischief bred.

Gair drwg anianol
A lusg ddrwg yn ei ol.

1558

Languor lasts for many a day,
When to death it is the way.

Hir nych i angeu.

1559

Asleep the brave man's rage will lie.
Till it be roused by battle-cry.

Bid war antur glew wrth awr.

1560

Unchecked by doubt,
A fool speaks out.

Blaengar ymadrawdd ffol.

1561

Drooping and withered soon is all,
On which an idler's breath can fall.

Mae anadl y diogi yn mallu pob peth y cwympo arno.

1562

The more the race of wolves increases,
The worse for those who carry fleeces.

Po amlaf fo'r bleiddiau gwaethaf fydd i'r defaid.

1563

The field will be green
Where an army hath been.

Bid las lluarth.

1564

Fate best befriended
Him who best ended.

Goreu tynged diwedd da.

1565

As clothes to warm, and meat to feed,
Nobility is made to lead.

Bonedd a dywys,
Dillad a gynnwys.

1566

Of the pure woman, and the morning bright,
The fame and splendour may be gone ere night.

Bore coch a mawredd gwraig.

1567

Where the line hath tightest strain,
There the line will part in twain.

Po tynnaf fo'r llinyn, cyntaf y tyr.

1568

Sooner a wolf's teeth from his jaw
Than malice from his heart you'll draw.

Hawdd tynu dannedd blaidd, ond hwyr y tynnir o hano ei anian.

1569

To seem unwilling is the task
For a maid whom none will ask.

Bid wastad wraig ni erchir.

1570

Wasteful he
Who salts the sea.

Bwrw heli yn y mor.

1571

Counsels which high matters weigh
Must outlast a winter's day.

Byrddydd ni dderfydd cynghor.

1572

To be short-lived is the fate
Of the man a saint doth hate.

Byrhoedlawg digasawg saint.

1573–1574

The man who is the devil's own
By these three tokens may be known,
Forbidding his concealment each :
His look, his bearing, and his speech.

Tri nod cywir y sydd ar ddyn y diawl : ac nis gall ymddchawraw
ag hwynt : ei air, ei olwg, ei ym modi.

1575

'Twill cost a scratch your cat to throw
Where cats must think it death to go.

Bwrw câth i gythraul.

1576

To go to mill, and meal to make,
Is all the meal that wretches take.

Melina tlawd ei gwynos.

1577

What you treasure most in mind,
'Mid the refuse look to find.

Cais yn y mwlwg.

1578

In the house a single child
Is a hundred pleasures mild.

Cant mwyn mab yn ty.

1579

Hateful reproach,
That we encroach.

Casbeth a oreilitio.

1580

Fold either arm, and close the fist,
Will knaves who nothing do nor list.

Cofl gwas diawg.

1581

The thoughtless only and the bold
Seek out a villain in his hold.

Ceisiaw diriad yn ei dyddyn.

1582

In taking right to grind, you take
What all men pay for grinding's sake.

Cafad malu cafad ei werth.

1583

He who in bonds is seen to stay,
But for his bonds would run away.

Cerddwys a rwymwys.

1584

Mares that are lame
Have foals the same.

Caseg gloff cloff ei hebol.

1585

By her chuckle you'll know when
To the barn hath got the hen.

Cogor iar yn ydlan.

1586

To warn a lion in like case,
Punish the bear before his face.

Cosbi yr arth y' ngwydd y llew.

1587

Holdfast may be always known
By the hardness of his bone.

Ci crâff caledach asgwrn.

1588

What for his own he knows, a man
Will tighter hold than pincers can.

Craffach no'r efail.

1589

Horse-laughter, by the general rule,
Will be the laughter of a fool.

Crechwen ar enau ynfyd.

1590

As dangerous, when sheathless made
A sword is, as it 's short in blade

Cuall cleddyf byr o wain.

1591

Man, who the earth with furrows galls
At last into a furrow falls.

Cwymp y gwr yn y rhych.

1592

Though many a good on earth there be,
One perfect good you'll never see.

Cyd boed da, nid gwirdda.

1593

However crafty it may be,
There's rashness still in villainy.

Cyd boed doeth diried ys drud.

1594

All would all the better thrive
If all their team afield would drive.

Cydles i bawb galw yr ychain.

1595

If horse-flesh you're compelled to eat,
'Tis fair to make the colt your meat.

Cyd ysso gig march bid ar gig ebol.

1596

In bargain's name a gift they take
Who with the generous bargain make.

Cyfnewid â hael.

1597

Happiness will ever last,
Till goodness shall away have passed.

Cyfoed fydd da a dedwydd.

1598

No secret apart
From the head hath the heart.

Cyfrin pen â chalon.

1599

A rag may ape
A napkin's shape.

Cynnelw cinyn gan gadechyn

1600

If you wish for distant sight,
Take your stand upon a height.

Cyrchid fryn a ddisgwylio.

1601

If with dog in fight you close,
Drop your cudgel on his nose.

Cyrch y ci ar y ffroen.

1602

The miser's meat
How sweet ! how sweet !

Chwegach bwyd cybydd.

1603

Who failure and disaster knows
Is readiest to come to blows.

Chwannog trwch i drin.

1604

While waves are weltering death around,
The fool is laughing, till he is drown'd.

Chwerthin a wna ynfyd yn boddi.

1605

The child that clamours most to roam
Will be the first to cry for home.

Chwannog mab i'w hynt,
Chwannog adref a fo cynt.

1606

When on a horse entire you set
A price, his perfect sex forget.

Cystal march a'i adfarchwerth.

1607

The beetle's flight
Announces night.

Chwil gan nos.

1608–1609

Should God on each man's forehead write
The name that would befit him quite,
The world could not supply a mask
To every man who one would ask.

Pei ysgryfenai Duw wir enw pob un ar ei dalcen pa le y ceid
defnydd mygwd i bawb a i ceisiai.

1610

Sinners the path to heaven show ;
The way-wise leave their way to go.

Dangos nêf i bechadur.
Dangos llwybr i gyfarwydd.

1611

God is merciful as strong,
And eternity is long.

Da yw Duw, a hir yw byth.

1612

Wouldst make a thong that's pointed well,
Begin the pointing from its swell.

Dechreu blaen carai o foly.

1613

Two parts in three of handsomeness
Hath one who wears a handsome dress.

Deuparth pryd ymdrwsiaw.

1614

One man twice brave, in reason's eyes,
Will count as two men of his size.

Drud a dal dau cyfled.

1615

Bliss will be rife
In blameless life.

Dibech fywyd gwyn ei fyd.

1616

All to a man should kindness show,
Though nothing more of him they know,
  If of his heart beguil'd
When looking on the earth's fair face,
Or work of beauty and of grace,
  Or on a little child.

Tri dyn y dylai bawb edrych yn hoff arnynt : sef, a ddysgwyl yn
serchawg ar wyneb y ddaiar; ar ymbwyll celfydd, ac ar blant
bychain.—*Bardic.*

1617

Unto the listless leave his trust
That help the unhelpful heaven must :
But this in thy remembrance bear,
That God doth for his cripples care.

Differo Duw diawg.
Duw yn borth i fusgrell.

1618

The violin's onflowing sweet,
With the harp's ecstatic beat,
Makes a joy that is complete.

Digon o grwth a thelyn.

1619

A dog for roving known, when found
Nine paces from your mansion's bound,
  Kill you may,
  And nothing pay.

Ci callawydd o'r lleddir naw cam i wrth y ty, ni thelir dim am
dano.

1620

Those who with water vessels fill,
Some water drops will surely spill.

Dir yw gadael peth o'r dwfr heibio.

1621

What history is you may divine
When pigs relate the feats of swine.

Son wrth foch am orchestion twrch.

1622

The thought of God's eternal mind
In human tongues its voice will find.

Duw a fedd, dyn a lefair.

1623

A promise once made
Is a debt to be paid.

Dyled ar bawb ei addaw.

1624

If silence can be overmuch,
The wisest man's excess is such.

Doeth dyn tra thawo.

1625

Two parts in three which make a town
Are the customs it doth own.

Deuparth tref ei harferau.

1626

Poor soul whose house shall managed be
By guests that live in it scot-free.

Drwg a drefna wrth ei drwyddedawg.

neu

Na ddal dy dŷ wrth gynghor dy drwyddedawg.

1627

God claims, all other claims above,
Justice, obedience, and love.

Tri phrif ofynion Duw : cariad ; cyfiawnder ; ac ufydd-dawd.

1628

Death's face is brass ; and brassier still
Will his be whom Death shall not kill.

Diwyl yw angeu,
Diwylach a edeu.

1629

That a poor boon you reckon may,
Which for its asking will not pay ;
And poor that place is which requires
More service than its guerdon hires.

Drwg yw'r peth, ni thal ei ofyn.
Drwg yw'r swydd ni thal ei gwasanaethu.

1630

Praise-all's praise
A smile will raise.

Chweirys gwawd o anianawd.

1631

Unless head know,
Tongue should not go.

Dywaid lafar ni wypo.

1632

As the whole nation must possess,
Little and great, the wilderness,
Upon the people's common green
No building rise, no plough be seen ;
Nor in the forest's common shade,
Of bush or tree be clearance made.

Ni ddylid adeilad y' ngobaith, aredig y' ngobaith, a digoediaw
tir gwyllt y' ngobaith.

1633

The freeman eats by choice and pleasure,
The captive by his dole and measure.

Dogn dyn o garchar.

1634
Over again will be begun
The work that once hath ill been done.

Drygwaith dwywaith y gwnair.

1635
No saints will last
A limekiln's fast.

Dirwest odyn.

1636
What a man to God hath given,
He gave but in exchange for heaven.

Duw a rannodd nef a gafodd.

1637
If on your knave your fists you use,
For years his hate you will not lose.

Dyrnod gwas
Hir yw ei gas.

1638
His friend from gripe of law assure,
His friend from lawless wrong secure,
The palace cook can, when he takes
In hand the first joint which he bakes,
Until the time when he doth bring
And set the last before the king.

Nawdd cog yw or pan bofo y golwyth cyntaf, hyd pan osoto y
diweddaf rhag bron y brenin.

1639
Good gold will pass wherever shown ;
The sterling man but where he's known.

Nid fal aur da ydd â y dyn.

1640
Scurvy, if but a glance he throw,
Will any scurvy creature know.

Edwyn crâch y llall.

1641

The summer's day that warms a king
Its comfort to a dog will bring.

Ef a ddaw hâf i gi.

1642

This earthly ball
Has room for all.

Eang yw y byd i bawb.

1643

A wicked man, the worse he be,
Fault in himself the less will see.

Ni wyl diriad arno fai.

1644

A hundred men upon the lea
Stand facing steel and gun ;
Let every one a hundred be,
And all the hundred one.

Elid un i gant, elid cant i un.

1645

The old wisewoman's dream but shows
Which way her inclination goes.

Breuddwyd gwrach wrth ei hewyllys.

1646

A man once losing his right mind
A wicked right hand soon will find.

Ehegr fydd dryglaw i anmhwyll.
neu
Disymmwth fydd dryglaw i anmhwyll.

1647

Gladly the crone will go to mill
In hopes her mouth thereat to fill.

Elid y wrach i'r freuan
Er ei genau ei hunan.

1648

Before your sack you open wide
Secure the pig to clap inside.

Egor dy gwd pan gaech borchell.

1649

When down the fatal deluge tears
Let ' Horror' be the name it bears.

Ergryn llwir lliaws addoed.

1650

High-couraged be he
Who would venturesome be.

Bid drud glew.

1651

Of an almsgiving you may brag
Whene'er the hungry tastes your stag.

Elusen tam o garw.

1652

Thrice o'er for insult he shall pay
Who with his neighbour's consort lay.

Tair gwaith y dychaifar sarâad gwr pan ymeer ei wraig.

1653

The ear of corn that's full of bread
Carries submissively its head ;
But stiff and straight as arrow quite
Stands that which grainless is and light.

Twysen lawn a estwng ei phen : twysen wag a saif yn syth.

1654

Woman's ill name is like a breeze
O'erblown to us from filthy lees.

Gair gwraig fal gwynt yn faweidiau.

1655

If left must one be in the lurch,
For the vilest make a search.

Os bydd neb yn ol bid y bawaf.

1656

To strangers he a good dog shows
Which treats the strangers as his foes.

Gelyn i ddyn ci da.

1657

About a desert you must roam
To find the faithless in his home.

Gnawd aelwyd ddiffydd yn ddiffaith.

1658

Aptest for vows from all to part
Is he who hath an empty heart.

Gnawd a fo digu diofryd.

1659

Not a villain you'll see
But a blemish hath he.

Gnawd anaf ar ddiriaid.

1660

The feeble and spare
Have acquaintance with care.

Gnawd ar eiddil ofalon.

1661

She and her patience have not parted
Who is a mother mother-hearted.

Ni cholles mam ammynedd.

1662

One bird in hand is twice as good
As the two plumpest in the wood.

Gwell aderyn mewn llaw no dau yn llwyn.

1663

A brawl into a fight hath grown
Where the arms have up been lifted,
Blows been given, flesh been rifted,
And through its gashes blood hath flown.

Sef yw ymladd, dyrchaf, a gosawd, a gwaed, a gweli.—*Laws.*

1664

Better it is to make delay
Because in banishment we roam,
Than from our business stop away
Because we've found a grave at home.

Gwell araws o alltudedd, nag araws o fedd.

1665

Give those who fail
Their leave to rail.

Hael yd gwyn pob colledig.

1666

To bards forbidden things through life
Are folly, indolence, and strife :
For bards pretend without pretence
To kindness, industry, and sense.

Tair deddf ochel y sydd ar fardd ; gochel diogi, can mai gwr wrth
ymgais ydyw; a gochel cynhen can mai gwr wrth heddwch
ydyw ; a gochel ffolineb can mai gwr wrth bwyll ydyw.—*Bardic.*

1667

None are so generous as they
Who nothing have to give away.

Hael byrllawiawg.

1668

The vicious cat whose claws you shore
Is twice as vicious as before.

Hanbid gwaeth y ddrygcath o dorri ei hewinedd.

1669

With true men by the wall you less forlorn are
Than with snug villains in the chimney corner.

Gwell am y pared a dedwydd, nag am y tan a diriaid.

1670

Who passes summer with the unhonour'd dead
Winters with blame and shame upon his head.

Haf hyd galan gauaf hyd fai.

1671

Your house's history to know
To the forest you must go.

Hanes ty hanes coed.

1672

Better noblesse
Than churlishness.

Gwell bonedd na thaeogrwydd.

1673

God's own goodness you will raise
To a higher pitch by praise.

Gwell Duw wrth ei folawd.

1674

Your awkward joiner's work untrue,
Less than your awkward smith's, you'll rue.

Gwell drygsaer na drygof.

1675

'Twixt eager gull and cunning cheat
The case is plain to the discreet.

Hawdd dyddio rhwng ffals a chwannog.

1676

If one the child remembers, he
Will by the man remember'd be.

Mab coff, gwr a'th coff.

1677

Bloody hands and bloody feet
Proof of killing make complete.

Lladd gwaed â'i ddwylaw ac â'i draed.

1678

If e'er a man shall marry one,
For a maid, who maid is none,
Let her shift, which best doth fit,
Behind her and before be slit.
Then in her grasp the tail be placed
Of his steer, greased with kitchen waste :
And if by strength of hand she can
Hold fast, and keep, what she doth span,
That steer, it is the law's decision,
Shall be that unmade maid's provision.

Or twyllforwyn a geffir heb wad, ei chrys a dorir tu rhagddi a thra
ei chefn, ac oddiyna ei gwr a ddyry iddi enderig gwedi iraw ei
losgwrn, ac o dichona hi ei attal herwydd ei losgwrn, cymered
hi ef yn ei hegweddi.—*Laws.*

1679

Better to find what nothing cost
Than lose what you would miss if lost.

Gwell caffael y nodwydd na cholli y cwlltr.

1680

An untaught urchin, for his game,
Will set his father's house aflame.

Mab heb ddysg,
Ty a lysg.

1681

Pleasure is there, and should be,
Little for malignity.

Meddiant bychan i ddrwg ewyllys.

R

1682

Many who sharp famine feel
Will begging go with dog at heel.

Llawer dyn mawr ei eisieu a eilw ei gi gydag ef.

1683

Better be lanky and be whole
Than sizeable by lop and poll.

Gwell cul cyfa na byr anghyfa.

1684

By the mill much water goes
Of which the miller nothing knows.

Llawer ddwfr a â heibio heb wybod i 'r melinydd.

1685

Better is a skilful trade
Than a fortune ready made.

Gwell creft no golud.

1686

Three punishments a Christian needs
    Inflict upon his foe :
Forgiveness ; silence ; and good deeds,
    Far as his power will go.

Tri cosb Cristion ar ei elyn : maddeu iddo ; tewi arno ; a gwneuthur daioni iddo hyd eithaf gallu.

1687

Such listening ears by none are lent
As by the man on learning bent.

Ni wrendy ond astud.

1688

A May that is as winter cold
Will warm the barns with what they hold.

Mai oer a wna ysgubor gynhes.

1689

No greater foe doth man beset
Than the riches he doth get.

Gelyn yw i ddŷn ei dda.

1690

He who a stag's head to the king,
Or but the tongue of anything,
Gives, to his judge a tongue shall bring ;
For he is judging, every day,
On all that every tongue can say.

Yr yngnad llys a gaiff dafawd y carw y del ei ben yn anrheg i'r
brenin ; ac y tafodau oll o'r llys a fo iawn eu hysu, canys yntau
a farn ar y tafodau oll.—*Laws.*

1691

To talk of mountains those avail
Who never will a mountain scale.

Haws dywedyd mynydd no myned drosto.

1692

No place for refuge can compete
With a courser train'd and fleet.

Hawdd nawdd ynghysgawd gorwydd.

1693

All earthly love he well forswears
For whom no earthly being cares.

Gnawd digu diofryd.

R 2

1694

'Time to go' is often said
To speed a journey that's ill sped.

Gnawd mynych awn i fethdaith.

1695

Better is the man of bone
Than he not out of gristle grown.

Gwell gwr no gwyr.

1696

When you to brutes your will express
A word is talking to excess.

Gormod iaith yw 'twt' ar farch.

1697

Little the farmer knows of ease,
Whose land his landlord daily sees.

Gwae a wyl ei arglwydd beunydd.

1698

Better review
Than battle true.

Gwell chwarae nog ymladd.

1699

Spirited he who in his cup
Puts all he has and drinks it up.

Hirfrydig a yfo ei holldda.

1700

The needy falling in your way,
Before he parts, has much to say.

Hir chwedl anghenawg.

1701

To build a part is harder found
Than to burn all unto the ground.

Haws llosgi y tŷ no 'i adeilad.

1702

After drink
The spirits sink.

Gnawd wedi llyn lledfrydedd.

1703

Oftenest, no doubt,
A theft comes out.

Gnawd lledrad yn ddiymgel.

1704

Sure then our knowledge is, and wide,
When being's sphere is throughly tried ;
And all we hold in recollection,
—Each accident and each affection,—
And are so fraught with circumspection,
That no experience is required
To traverse any world desired.
And such the knowledge is we gain
Ere we the blissful sphere attain.

Tri chadernyd gwybodaeth darfod treiglaw pob cyflwr bywyd,
cofiaw treiglaw pob cyflwr, a'i ddamwain ; a gallu treiglaw pob
cyflwr fal y mynner ar prawf a barn, a hyn a geir yn ngylch y
gwynfyd.—*Bardic.*

1705

Watch a bad man, and you'll see
That his luck as bad will be.

Gnawd aflwydd gan ddiriaid.

1706

The meatiest joints of all the cheer
Still in the eating disappear.

Ni phery cig bras yn wastad.

1707

The simple seldom has the skill
His cup of vengeance full to fill.

Gnawd dial anghwbl gan anghelfydd.

1708

Where a cross rises from the ground
Oft may a resting-place be found.

Gnawd gorphwysfa lle bo croes.

1709

Of frequent, secret, close approaches
Will come at last the world's reproaches.

Gnawd gwarth o fynych gyswyn.

1710

The King's chief huntsman none shall cite
Unless he find him in the night,
Or find him rising in the morn
Before his buskins on are drawn.

Y pencynydd, oni cheffir cyn ei gyfodi o'i wely, a gwisgaw ei
gwranau, ni ddyly ateb i neb o'r hawl a ofyner iddo.—*Laws.*

1711

Its sweetest meat a joint supplies
Where nearest to the bone it lies.

Melysaf y cig, po nesaf i'r asgwrn.

1712

Thin is the hare
On a field that is bare.

Llymaf y maes
Llymaf yr ysgyfarnog.

1713

Default will the performance be
Of what a woman promis'd thee.

Gnawd eddewid gwraig waith ryphall.

1714

'Tis something, to be kept alive,
But quite another thing to thrive.

Llawer rhwng byw a digon.

1715

The country where most love you find
Will be the country to your mind.

Lle da pob lle y carer.

1716

Others at your discretion trust ;
Your wife's dad's daughter—when you must.

Na chred fyth ferch dy chwegrwn.

1717

Let dogs that sleep
Their slumbers keep.

Na ddeffro y ci, a fo'n cysgu.

1718

What man hath need should be supplied,
God for his journey will provide.

Gosymdaith dyn Duw a'i rhan.

1719

The corn its direst ravage knows
When fellow-countrymen are foes.

Gwaethaf i'r yd rhyfel teisban.

1720

The worst thing you can keep in store
Will be the daughter on your floor.

Gwaethaf ystor o ferch.

1721

Bad is his case who, in the stage
Of youth, is longing for old age.

Gwae ieuangc a eiddun henaint.

1722

Often to, and often fro,
Herdsman bad will come and go.

Mynych addaw drwg fugail.

1723

To lie upon his mistress' lap
Is a puppy's happiest hap.

Llon colwyn ar arffed ei feistres.

1724

One crippled wolf will worse be found
Than any two wolves that are sound.

Gwaeth un blaidd cloff no dau iach.

1725
No leech so sure,
As time, to cure.

Nid meddyg ond amser.

1726
Drain'd of force and reft of fire
Is the slave of low desire.

Digraid pawb drythyll.

1727
The kid on which at birth you dote
Daily worsens to a goat.

Gwaethwaeth fal mab gafr.

1728
No profit by your pains you make
When, serving others, pains you take.

Ni chynnydd gweinid arall.

1729
The hairs that first their colour lose,
The rest, as colourless, accuse.

Gwallt bonwyn a gwyn estronion.

1730
He, who would not, when he could ;
Is not able when he would.

Ni fyn, pan gaffo, ni chaiff pan fyno.

1731
No burden's weight,
As age, so great.

O bob trwm trymmaf henaint.

1732

Little trouble need you take,
When a scald-head you would break.

Hawdd torri ben crach.

1733

Those who no means have to prepare
Are always taken unaware.

Anmharawd pob anallu.

1734

Better it is arriving late
Than coming early but to wait.

Gwell gan hwyr na chan foreu.

1735

No eulogium e'er can lift
Your soul so high as will your shrift.

O bob ceinmyged cyffes oreu.

1736

By grievous word
Is anger stirred.

Gair garw a gyffry ddigofaint.

1737

See that thy bearing ne'er belies
His thought who on thy truth relies.

Na fydd frad fygel i'r a'th greto.

1738

Often may you trust your life,
Your secret never, to your wife.

Na fid dy wraig dy gyfrin.

1739

All who sing,
Both great and small,
Our brothers all
Who sing we call.

Brodyr pob cerddorion.

1740

Curses which men, as deadly, fear,
The miser long survives to hear.

Hir fydd i gybydd ei gabl.

1741

Distant performance is, and slow,
Where all the promise hath been 'No.'

Hir eddewid i nâg.

1742

Good reason to dispute as any,
' Penniless ' hath for a penny.

Mal yr anghenawg am ei geiniawg.

1743

Long runs, e'er fate applies her shears,
The thread of a thin woman's years.

Hir fydd edau gwraig eiddil.

1744

To him who builds in open field,
Three timbers must the woodland yield :
Two pillars stout the roof to rear ;
One mighty beam to hold its gear.
And these to part with or refuse
The woodland's ranger cannot choose.

Tri phren a ddyly pob adeilwr maesdir eu caffael gan y neb a
   bieuffo y coed,—myno y coedwr na myno onid amgen ;—nenbren
   a dwy nen ffyrch.—*Laws.*

1745
When the flood aloud doth roar
Your feudal lord lays in his store.

Cell arglwydd y weilgi.

1746
The Irishman once in, a bout
Of tugs and blows must get him out.

Mal Gwyddel am ei yru allan.

1747
Let other foes your lord attack ;
But join them when he turns his back.

Gwell erlid arglwydd na'i ragod.

1748
There is nought but fate existing :
Fate is nought but God subsisting.

Nid bod, ond angen ; nid angen ond Duw.

1749
Better by wedding to bestow
Thy wealth, than wealth to wedding owe.

Gwell gan wraig a fo da genthi, nag a fo da iddi.

1750
No looking-glass can help the blind ;
To see yourself look on your kind.

Drych i bawb ei gymmydawg.

1751
When cunning hands from nature swerve,
A stone may wanton uses serve.

Drythyll maen yn llaw esgud.

1752

You'll folly find
Of many a kind.

Llawer math sydd a 'or ynfydrwydd.

1753

'Tis never an unpleasant task,
Of one who loves us, boon to ask.

Hawdd eiriawl ar a garer.

1754

Shiftiness, debauch, and brawl
Would make villains of us all.

Tri gorefras dirieidi : glythineb ; ymladd ; ac anwadalwch.

1755

To an old man never lift
Thy voice soliciting a gift.

Rhodd i hen nag adolwg.

1756

You need not have been long at school
To turn the tables on a fool.

Hawdd talu ffug i ffol.

1757

Hardly one sufferer in a score
Will keep his hand from off his sore.

Llaw pawb ar ei anaelau.

1758

If a dog with bones you pelt,
The pain and insult are not felt.

Ni chwyn ci er ei daro ag asgwrn.

1759

Trivial accidents are free
From the bond of fate's decree.

Nid i bob amddawd tynged.

1760

The Gael will tug
To keep his rug.

Mal y Gwyddel am y ffaling.

1761-2

To him man's eye unbidden goes
Whom he for a protector knows.
But God on him his eye will turn
Whom all men for a wretch discern.

Golwg dyn ar a'i dyhudd.
Golwg Duw ar adyn.

1763

Small is the grief repentance brings
When we repent of selling things.

Goreu edifeirwch edifeirwch gwerth.

1764

Off from amongst us was he borne,
To the sound of pipe and horn.

Ef a aeth hynny ar gyrn a phibau.

1765

Hardly slacks
Fire in flax.

Mal y tan yn y carth.

1766

Rarely the cudgels up he'd take,
And never for another's sake.

Ni chymmerai cogel am ei gâr.

1767

Woe to all beneath a roof
Which never echoed a reproof.

Gwae y ty, nas clywer llais cerydd.

1768

A dog his fellow dog will leave
And to his fellow's master cleave.

Y gwn a rhod i gannwr ac nid a'r gwn o dy'r gwr.

1769

He is invited to the curd
Who of the cheese has nothing heard.

Efe a fydd am y maidd, a'r ni fu am y caws.

1770

Gifts around in showers to fling,
Is the manner of a king.

Gnawd rhiau eu rhadau yn wasgarawg.

1771

Let God take away,
In a trice to repay.

Dyccid Duw, daphar o law.

1772

'Tis a furious passion's fate
Often to conclude in hate.

Gnawd rhygas gwedi rhyserch.

1773

Could fowls about religion parley,
You'd find that they believe in barley.

Crefydd iar wrth ei gylfin.

1774

Fame will last
When life is past.

Hwy clod na hoedl

1775

An inextricable heap
Lies bloodstain on a sheep.

Bydd hyfagl gwyar ar oen.

1776

Whatever follows to alloy,
Intoxication's self is joy.

Bid llawen meddw.

1777

If one unto his lawful king
Proud word or rough shall say,
The atoning fine
Of three fat kine
That pert one twice shall pay.

Y neb, a ddywetto yn syberw, neu yn hagr wrth y brenin, taled deir bu camlwrw yn ddeuddyblig am hynny.—*Laws.*

1778

The more a man in wisdom grows,
The less of morning sleep he knows.

Ni chwsg dedwydd hun fore.

1779

Follow still
Lovers will.

Gnawd serchog ymlyniad.

1780

No counsel given upon earth
Will like your father's merit heed ;
No prayers are utter'd from your birth
That like your mother's intercede.

Nid cynghor ond tad ;
Nid gweddi ond mam.

1781

The devil and God's human friend
But slowly their acquaintance mend.

Ni chymmydd diawl a dwywawl.

1782

Many first cousins make their cousin strong :
His list of second cousins is but long.

Nid galluawg ond cefnderw ;
Nid cenhedlawg ond cyfyrdyr.

1783

There is no battle without pains ;
And every death a tear constrains.

Nid brwydr ond gwewyr.
Nid lladd ond dager.

1784

Nor often nor soon
Will you meet a poltroon.

Na fynych gwr llwfr.

1785

You'll never get to work and stand
The mill that's made to work in hand.

Ni wastatâ mwy no breuan dinfoel.

1786

Where open lies forbidden ground,
There God upon the watch is found.

Ni chwsg Duw pan rydd gwared.

1787

In a moment dumb is made
The chatterer, when he's afraid.

Mud arynaig y llafar.

1788

Stars alone are things untold :
Nothing as the moon is cold.

Nid amlder ond sêr.
Nid oer ond lleuad.

1789

Wistful is the sight of grain
From which the starving must refrain.

Hir grawn gan newyn.

1790

Long on your legs will better fit
Life's purposes, than long to sit.

Gwell byr eistedd no byr sefyll.

1791

From the jaw his beard did stream
Like a web from weaver's beam.

Mal yr eddi am y garfan.

1792

When honour unto thee is shown
Unask'd for, take it as thine own.

Na wrthod dy barch pan y cynnycier.

1793

I must to him next neighbour be
Who is next neighbour unto me.

Nesaf i bawb ei nesaf.

1794

Nearer sits my shirt to me
Than my coat can ever be.

Nes i mi fy nghrys nâ'm pais.

1795
He who to court without an office went,
Back from the court in office should be sent
A el i lys heb neges doed a'i neges ganto.

1796
You're better a wretch's prayers deserving
Than the mightiest master serving.
Gwell bendith y tlawd nâ meistrolaeth y cadarn.

1797
Congenial place, companion kind,
In water only ships can find.
Croesaw dur i long.

1798
The false oath slips
Through filthy lips.
Aflan genau anudonawl.

1799
Of herdsmen he is not the best
Who is often on the quest.
Arofyn drwg fugail.

1800
The proof of theft which all believe in
Is to catch the thief a thieving.
Arwaesaf i leidr ei ddal.

1801
Those who their wages ask for earn them ;
And none but undeservers spurn them.
A ddyfo i dorth a'i dyhaith
Ef a ddyfydd a wnel ei waith.

1802

Never savage
Yet was seen
That was modest
Or was clean.

Aflednais pob gwyllt.

1803

Better is he, almost a mite,
Than she that is a mountain quite.

Gwell migwrn o wr, no mynydd o wraig.

1804

In every bosom darkly dwells
A messenger whose whisper tells.

Aneglur genad yw ceudawd.

1805

Long is the meal
With a knife not of steel.

Hir saig a chyllell aflem.

1806

No villain cares
What oath he swears.

Ni ddawr diriad pa dyng.

1807

If longing for an invitation,
Appear too ill for acceptation.

A fynno gymhell bid claf.

1808

Herlyn in battle takes to flight
Because he longs again to fight.

Nid unwaith y caed Herlyn.

1809

Better have but one ploughshare
Than of cow-posts own a pair.

Gwell un crywyn no dau fuddelw.

1810

No little pleasure, and no hurt,
A fox will take from his own dirt.

Hoff gan fadyn ei faw ei hun.

1811

A lodger if obliged to take,
A woman is the choice you'll make.

Gwell gwestai gwraig nog un gwr.

1812

The appointed palace judge shall swear
By relic and by altar, there,
Never, never, while he live,
Wrong judgment knowingly to give.

Dyly yr yngnad llys dyngu ar y crair ac ar yr allawr aci wneithaid
a ddoter ar yr allawr na farno gam farn byth hyd y gwypo.—
Laws.

1813

The liveliest evening that we spend
Hastens the swiftest to its end.

Gorddiweddid hwyr fuan.

1814

The madman deems a pleasant thing
The bludgeon he is flourishing.

Hoff gan ynfyd ei gnwpa.

1815

Be highest praise
To gentle ways.

Goreu cynneddfau cadw moes.

1816

By light can never man be led
Like that which from his brain is shed.

Goreu canwyll pwyll i ddyn.

1817

Better arrive on Christmas day
Than keep for the whole year away.

Gwell gwr a ddaeth ymhen y flwyddyn, nâ'r gwr ni ddaeth byth.

1818

Never yet by any cur
Was I barked at as by her.

Mwy nag un ci a'm cyfarthodd i.

1819

You wish your slave nor good nor evil
When you wish him at the devil.

Bwrw caeth i gythraul.

1820

My father and my mother kiss'd,
And then their way to church they miss'd.

Mi a gawn a fai gan fy mam, ac ni chawn a'i dygai i'r llan.

1821

He who after feasting goes
Likes horseback better than his toes.

Marchawg a fydd wedi gwyl.

1822-3

None can match a child in wishes ;
None so clean are as the fishes.

Nid chwannog ond mab.
Nid glan ond y pysg.

1824

A man who will the honey take,
The sting must suffer for its sake.

Mèl a'i gola.

1825

The foot which is with walking sore
But worse becomes by walking more.

Nac ir gwadn hanbyd gwaeth.

1826

Those who of wealth no means can show,
Their wealth to wrong or fairies owe.

Byw ar dir y tylwyth teg.

1827

All horsemen riding rod can show,
None go afoot without a bow.

Nid marchawg heb ffon ;
Nid peddestr heb fwa.

1828

From every point in heaven's wide sphere
Winds bring a downfall when they veer.

O bob ffordd o'r awyr, ydd ymchwelo y gwynt, y daw gwlaw.

1829

The kite that can outspeed his prey,
Owes to his leanness that he may.

Paham y bydd cûl y barcud? Am ysglyfiad.

1830

Better unwelcome truth reveal'd
Than truth by welcome lie conceal'd.

Gwell gwir na chelwydd.

1831

The stone, that is too hard and thick
To break, a cunning dog will lick.

Paham y llyf y ci y maen? Am nas gall ei ysu.

1832

No single tree
Can a forest be.

Nid ellir coed o unpren.

1833

Where man in closest straits is bound,
God amplest freedom sees around.

Po ingaf gan ddyn eangaf fydd gan Dduw.

1834

Where no good reason can avail her,
Be sure excuses will not fail her.

Ni ddiffyg esgus ar wraig.

1835

Better is 'Alas for me,'
Than 'How miserable we.'

Gwell wae fi nâ ni.

1836

Corn in a glove you'll gather more
Than in a bag from door to door.

Gwell i'r gwr a aeth â maneg i yta nog a ffetan.

1837

To fame no mortal can attain
While his detractors hearing gain.

Ni fawrheir tra oganer.

1838

If the herdsman's heart be glad,
Of the household none are sad.

O bydd llawen y bugail, llawen fydd y tylwyth.

1839

With whom, and when, and how, and where.
The good-for-nothing has small care.

Ni ddawr puttain pa gnuch.

1840

When thou standest under weight,
See, oh see, thou standest straight.

Pan bwyser arnad tyn dy droed attat.

1841

Two less are elements than seven :
Water, and earth, air, fire, and heaven.
From the four first come all things dead ;
Life from the last, and God, are bred :
And thus, by mingling all the five,
Come all things lifeless and alive.

Pump tywarchen y sydd : sef, daiar ; dwr ; tan ; awyr ; a nef : ac
o'r pedair cyntaf pob defnydd difywyd, ac o'r nef Duw a phob
bywydawl ; ac o ymgyd y pump hyn pob peth ai bywydawl
ai anmywydawl.—*Bardic.*

1842

Though all around
Be prone to theft,
Skim milk is found
Where it was left.

Pa le yn y fuddai y mae yr enwyn.

1843

When thy game's too good to mend,
Bring the playing to an end.

Pan fo tecca 'r chware, goreu fydd peidio.

1844

'Tis wrong to feel
Toe above heel.

O bydd uwch bawd, na sawdl.

1845

Some skill will it show
To conceal what you know.

Gwaith celfydd celu rhin.

1846

Quick to feel, and to resent,
Is the man of high descent.

Hawdd peri i foneddig sori.

1847

A house you call a house in vain
If no man it doth contain.

Nid tŷ heb wr.

1848

A leaping pole will never come
Kindly with you in your thumb.

Nid â bawd yd ddyfnir llâth hir.

1849

No dullard but must lazy be ;
Nor lazy, but a sinner he.

Nid diawg ond syrthni,
Nid syrthni ond pechod.

1850

When blind to blind
His guidance lends,
In some deep pool
Their journey ends.

Pan dywyso y dall ddal arall, y ddau a ddygwydd i'r pwll.

1851

If plotters there be more than two,
There will be a rendezvous.

Gnawd yn y bo cydwyr, y bydd cyrch.

1852

Better my dog range wild and wide
Than sit and settle by my side.

Gwell ci a rodio, na chi a eisteddo.

1853

When first a favourite strain you hear,
Know 'twill find favour but a year.

Ni phara cywydd namyn un flwyddyn.

1854

Message from a great man take
Message to a great man bring ;
And the profit you will make
Is the honour of the thing.

Neges pendefig yn rhad.

1855

No blemish you'll name
Like merited blame.

Gwaethaf anaf anfoes.

1856

Impudent rogue ! on God he'd palm
A dead monk off, without a qualm.

Sommi Duw â mynach marw.

1857

Where you some riches once have found,
Give freely, and they will abound.

Yn y lle y bo y da,
Y rhoir, ac y tycia.

1858

He who a horse has of his own
Is welcome to a horse on loan.

Y neb, a fo a march ganddo, a gaiff farch ym menthyg.

1859

Let not daylight's care be cast
On the dream with night o'erpast.

Elid bryd yn ol breuddwyd.

1860

A hog that's squealing
The knife is feeling.

Yr hwch a wich ys hi a lâdd.

1861

Only a fool will think me wise
His rugged wrapper to despise.

Ynfyd a gabl ei wrthban.

1862

Black was the grain
Of the goat that is slain.

Yr afr ddu a las.

1863

Who nothing stake
Small gain can make.

Odid elw heb antur.

1864

Out of five score you'll scarcely see
One who can a companion be.

Odid o'r cant cydymmaith.

1865

All his powers to understand,
Needs a stranger in the land.

Oedd rhaid deall i alltud.

1866

That with his office is invested
The palace judge, his gifts make known :
    First comes a chess-board from the king,
Carved out of some sea monster's bone ;
    Next from the queen a golden ring ;
The like from the court-bard alone.
And shame it were, while life doth stay,
That these he sold, or gave away.

Y brawdwr llys a ddyly oferdlysau pan wystler ei swydd iddo : nid
amgen tawlbwrdd o asgwrn morfil, i gan y brenin ; a modrwy
aur i gan y frenines ; ac arall i gan y bardd teulu ; ac yr oferdlysau
hyny ni ddyly efe nac eu rhoddi nac eu gwerthu tra byddo byw.

1867

There's none beside
A swan for pride

Nid balch ond alarch.

1868

Better to suspect and spare,
Than swallow greedily, your share.

Gwell rhan ofni nâ rhan lyncu.

1869

None so poor is as the wretch
Whom sickness on his bed doth stretch.

Nid tlodi ond clefyd.

1870

Want of sense is at the root
Of contentious dispute.

Nid gwall synwyr ond ymryson.

1871

Nought so barren is as sadness ;
Nought such genius hath as gladness.

Nid diddim ond trist.
Nid athrylyth ond llawen.

1872

Better the grasping hand of law
Than the ravening robber's claw

Gwell yw dirwy nag anrhaith.

1873

Thy priest respect
And keep thy friend :
Him thou'lt expect
To smooth thine end.

Na ddifanw dy beriglawr.

1874

Just where the path grows free and wide,
I turn not from my way aside.

Ni throaf yn fy ammwlch.

1875

Slow grows what grows at slower pace
Than grass within a market place.

Ni thyf egin yn marchnad.

1876

He who to robbers doth betray,
As arrant robber is as they.

Nid gwell i'r rhoddwr, nag i'r lleidr.

1877

Modesty will seldom speed
The modest—in his hour of need.

Nid gwiw gwylder rhag eisiau.

1878

Sweet is sin in consummation ;
Bitter in its expiation.

Nid melus ond pechod.
Nid chwerw ond penyd.

1879

He who goeth to and fro
Never can be said to go.

Nid myned a ddel eilwaith.

1880

A man there was of absent mind
Who rode the mare he rode to find.

Y gwr yn ceisio ei gaseg a'i gaseg dano.

1881

Small wit he broaches
Who vents reproaches.

Nid amwys a wnel gwarth.

1882

A blazing hearth and wintry day
Invite the visitor to stay.

Aelwyd a gymhell.

1883

A cock, though bold and hungry he,
Finds it no catch to catch a bee.

Ni lwydd gwenyn i geiliog.

1884

You may reasonably boast
The marrow taken from a post.

Nid hawdd tynnu mêr o bost.

1885

Let not those who love and long,
Go where trees are thick and strong.

Nid aeth rhyhir i goed.

1886

To each man is his heart a shrine ;
And he a priest to The Divine.

Oferen pawb yn ei galon.

1887

Nothing is so sure to be
As the instant certainty.

Sicraf yw yr hyn sicraf.

1888

Pibble pabble, tittle tattle,
As much as curly-pate doth prattle.
Tittle tattle, pibble pabble,
As much as doth the puppet gabble.

Siared cymmaint a mab saithcudyn.
Siared cymmaint a Merddin ar bawl.

1889

Wipe not from remembrance clean
Any friendship that hath been.

Nid anghof brodyrdde.

1890

All feel a thirst
For being first.

Pawb a chwennych anrhydedd.

1891-2-3-4

No fraud can like the world deceive us ;
At nought like death we grieve ;
No pain there is till hell receive us,
No bliss till heaven retrieve.

Nid twyll ond y byd.
Nid prudd-der ond marwolaeth.
Nid llawenydd ond nef.
Nid anhyfryd ond uffern.

1895

On him, who in a God believes,
Three privileges faith bestows :
Enough for this life he receives ;
Peace with his conscience he retrieves ;
And linked with heaven on earth he goes

Tri pheth a gaiff dyn o gredu yn Nuw : a fo raid yn y byd ; heddwch cydwybod, ac ymgyd a 'r nefawl.—*Bardic.*

1896
'Tis better that our sore should stay,
Than through our meddling go away.
Gwell mefl fod, no mefl gerdded.

1897
To wethers nothing will restore
The muscle which they had of yore.
Lleddid mollt ni ddyfydd.

1898
As in a couple hound and hound,
So man and wife are still at strife
Because they are in couple bound.
Mal cwn yn gyfreion.

1899
Better be lodged within a hut
Than from a castle be outshut.
Gwell tufewn fwth no thufaes castell.

1900
He who thinks to hide his plunder
By his arm, doth greatly blunder.
Syrthid mefl o gesail.

1901
The shovel that the muck should clear
Oft lies in muck o'er head and ear.
Mal rhaw yn miswal.

1902
Fraud with success will seldom meet
When it is practised on a cheat.
Nid twyll twyllo twyllwr.

1903

Never has lord an evil name
But he as vassal had the same.

Nid drwg arglwydd namyn drwg was.

1904

Whatever tail a dog can show,
It ne'er will make a buffalo.

Ni bydd bual o losgwrn y ci.

1905

None shall for his own behoof
Make me his hat or waterproof.

Ni byddaf na thoryn dwyn no chappan gwlaw.

1906

High and deep
Make slope or steep.

Ni bydd allt heb waered.

1907

All your agility 'twill bother
From one horse-back to back another.

Ni bu esgynnu gorwydd oddiar geffyl.

1908

When the dog has met disaster,
Distraction falls upon the master.

Pan wypo dyn lladd ci
Cynddaredd a yr arno.

1909

Climbs the cat worse with claws as shorn
Than with his claws as he was born?

Pa waeth y dring cath ar ol tori ei ewinedd?

1910

Give alms you may
On holiest day.

Nid oes gwyl rhag elusen.

1911

Every man that you can hail
Will ask your news and tell his tale.

Pawb a'i chwedl gantho.

1912

Better your ignorance to show
Than never asking never know.

Oni byddi cyfarwydd cyfarch.

1913

An evil, be sure,
An evil must cure.

Drwg ys dir rhag drwg.

1914

No sooner puss the mouse hath slain
Than she will worry it again.

O lladd y gath lygoden ar frys hi a'i hys ei hun.

1915

A foreman carpenter must be
The man who owns a property.

Pensaer pob perchennawg.

1916

Better old, and single still,
Than to have been wedded ill.

Gwell hir weddwdod no drwg briod.

1917

How to bite
The grass aright
Dutiful lambs
Will teach their dams.

Yr oen yn dysgu i'r ddafad bori.

1918

'Tis so, and pity be it should,
A bad wife makes a husband good.

Nid drygwr wrth ddrygwraig.

1919

Better for you are cats that roam
Than cats that with you make their home

Pei y gâth fyddai gartref, gwaeth fyddai i chwi.

1920

A child amongst the children smallest,
When man with men, o'ertops the tallest.

Mab ryvech pennid,
Talwys a ryfeichwys.

1921

Unless a leek is to be had,
Cook as you may, the sauce is bad.

Oni cheffi gennin, dwg fresych.

1922

She who weds near enough to know
Whene'er her father's cock doth crow,
A wifelike conduct will not show.

Ni bydd moesawg merch, a glyw lêf ceiliog ei thâd.

1923

O strive not to make
　　Things quite to your will,
For the tightest will break,
　　And the fullest will spill,
And the highest will fall
　　To the lowest of all.

Rhy dyn a dyr.
Rhy lawn a gyll.
Rhy uchel a syrth.

1924

Woe to the wretch whose evil trade
Hath a hundred wretched made.

Gwae undyn a wnel cant trist.

1925

The harder was the tug to thee,
The greater is thy victory.

Po mwyaf y trafod, mwyaf y gorfod.

1926

Better are verses writ in measure
Than lopp'd and lengthen'd at your pleasure.

Gwell can mesur na chan trwch.

1927

Man's cares, be sure
That God will cure.

Gofal dŷn Duw a'i gweryd.

1928

Of all the good things she possess'd,
My mother's ferule was the best.

Goreu gan fy mam ei lladd.

1929

Bolts are barrier slighter far
Than unfriendly feelings are.

Traws pawb lle ni charer.

1930

Strong as a giant though one be,
A weakling at his end is he.

Pob cadarn gwan ei ddiwedd.

1931

He deals in lies
Who prophesies.

Pob darogan dydderpid.

1932

Sell not thou what none will prize
Because it is of little size.

Na werth er bychodedd.

1933

As the more your home you near,
Louder and louder be your cheer.

alias,

Ever clearer as more near
To the homestead comes the cheer.

Nesnes y llefain i'r dref.

1934

The prophet whom the world receives,
None in his neighbourhood believes.

Nês nâ choel.

1935

Tell me not there can be supplied
To an old cow a new inside.

Newydd bennyg yn henfon.

1936

If at high meeting, when its task
Is finished, one a song shall ask,
A bard of Britain first shall sing
A hymn to God, a lay for king :
Then be the household bard desired
To sing the song that is required.

Pan fyner canu cerdd, y bardd cadeiriawg a ddyly ddechreu a'r
canu cyntaf o Dduw, a'r ail o 'r brenin bieufo y llys.   Gwedy y
bardd cadeiriawg y bardd teulu biau ganu y trydydd canu o
gerdd amgen.

1937

A numskull to match
Is a herring to catch.

Newid y penweig.

1938

If his cross-bow but once he bend,
A fool his bolt is sure to spend.

Buanyb saetha ynfyd ei follt.

1939

No bird is slow
Its mate to know.

Pob edn a edwyn ei gymmar.

1940

Hold but fast a single bone,
And the body is your own.

Un asgwrn a dâl.

1941

The blessing given in mistake
With it will not a blessing take.

Ni llwydd bendith, ni haedder.

1942

Cloth the best that there can be,
Is the reddest you can see.

Goreu o'r brethyn y cochaf.

1943

A body by excess abused
Can for no nobler ends be used.

Ni lwydd hil corph o anniweir.

1944

Cowards in vain
To refuge fly :
Those death escape
Who death defy.

Ni nawdd eing rhag llaith :
Engid glew o'i gyfarwaith.

1945

To sing and sing, where'er it goes,
Is all the toil a cuckoo knows.

Nid mwy gwaith côg nâ chanu.

1946

If the health be free from taint,
Well we wonder at complaint.

Iach rhydd rhyfedd pa gwyn.

1947

Penury is hardly cured
By hardships hardily endured.

Ni nawdd caledi rhag bychodedd.

1948

A fire but slowly up you draw,
Blowing with porridge in your jaw.

Nid hawdd chwythu tan a blawd yn ngenau.

1949

Blaming what skill and care combined
To make, you pick the hole you find.

Nid hawdd difenwi cywraint.

1950

Fees from all strangers passing through ;
Fees that on sudden death are due ;
The infant's custody, acquired
With heriot, from a man expired;
All that upon the waste doth stray;
All that the sea doth cast away;
All that the convict thief possesses;
All that as fine the Law assesses,
    The king shall hold
    To yield him gold.

Wyth pynfarch brenin y sydd : mor ; a diffaith ; ac achanawg
gwlad arall yn cerdded tir y brenin ; a lleidr ; marw yn swrth,
y brenin biau ran y marw o'r da oll, ac ni chaiff ddim o dda 'r
wraig a'r meibion ; anfab marw y caffo ebediw : camgylus y
caffo ddirwy neu gamlwrw i gantho.—*Laws.*

1951

Better as mendicant to roam
'Tis, than of hunger die at home.

Bu well i gwr a grwydrws nog a fu farw rhag newyn.

1952
Nothing brings a rich man joy
Like the birth of his first boy.
Nid hoffder ond etifedd.

1953
Where gentleman none is, to grace
The board, some snob takes highest place.
O eisiau gwrda y dodir bawddyn ar y bwrdd.

1954
Simple is the man that will
Buy a woodcock by his bill.
Nid wrth ei big y mae prynu cyffylawg.

1955
Empty bugbear,
Glittering bubble,
This world's pleasure !
This world's trouble !
Nid ydyw y byd ond bychydig.

1956
Though fancy for a knave beset you,
Love him his baseness will not let you.
Ni âd diriaid ei garw.

1957
If to the fire, day after day,
The pipkin go to heat its clay,
The day will come when, as before,
Pipkin to fire can go no more.
Hyd yn oed yr undydd ydd â'r crochan ar y tân.

1958

Poor is th' inheritance men take,
When to their lord they homage make.

Nid treftad anrhydedd arglwydd.

1959

Ill wakes a lawsuit which has slept ;
And worse a blood-feud overkept.

Gwell hen hawl nâ hen alanas.

1960

Bold are cowards when they jeer
The coward who has shown his fear.

Hy pawb yn absen ofn.

1961

You must creep
Before you leap.

Rhaid yw cropian cyn cerdded.

1962

Save me the man, a share receiving,
And not the share he would be leaving.

Gwell gwr no'i ran.

1963

Gentle the sway
Which many obey.

Gweithred llary llywiaw nifer.

1964

Hope not two sons-in-law to gain,
Unless you father daughters twain.

Nid hawdd deuddaw o'r unferch.

1965

Fools wait to find the post but slow
In coming, e'er to it they go.

Nid â post ar ynfyd a'r ynfyd a ddaw ar y post.

1966

If the free man a slave shall beat,
Twelve pennies down the case will meet :
Six the white home-spun cloth will bring,
To make him coat for cutting ling ;
Three more his leggings will provide ;
His gauntlets one, and boots beside ;
Two bill and axe will furnish well,
The hedge to pleach and tree to fell.

O tery dyn rhydd gaeth, taled iddo ddeuddeg ceiniawg cyfraith :
chwech i'r tair cyfelin o frethyn gwyn i wneuthur pais iddo wrth
ladd eithin.—*Laws.*

1967

Or win respect,
Or bear neglect.

Ni llwydd rhewfidd i ddiwaid.

1968

For salad to your sideboard go ;
To the tavern, news to know.

Tabler i lysau ;
Tafarn i chwedlau.

1969

Before you get your grass a-growing,
Your horse unto the dogs is going.

Y march a fydd marw tra fo'r gwellt yn tyfu.

1970

For meat you will not overpay
When purchasing the beast you flay.

Pryn tra flingych.

1971

Catastrophe is nighest
When pride is at highest.

Gnawd wedi traha, trangc hir.

neu
Pob traha yn y gorphen.

1972

He is poorly preferr'd,
Whose share is a third.

Rhan druan rhan draian.

1973

'Tis no true message you send out
If with it there shall go a doubt.

Nid neges heb farch.

1974

Dog's flesh never long will be
Down the gorge of you or me.

Nid mi nid ti
Llewad cig y ci.

1975

In so much stead
  Will nothing stand,
As comrade's head
  And comrade's hand.

Nid ymddiried ond cydymaith.

1976

He ascertains
Who takes the pains.

Nid ysbys ond a ymofynno.

1977

If he with whom the haft remains
Of his axe's theft complains,
Him the possessor of the axe
With his handle's theft will tax.

Sieffrai pieu 'r troed,
Sieffrai pieu 'r fwyall.

1978

A fool's advice may bring success;
And wisest heads may make a mess.

Ef a gair cynghor gan ynfyd,
Ef a gair gwall ar y callaf.

1979

By your dog 'twill be imparted
When you meet a man faint-hearted.

Rhybudd ofnawg a dal y ci.

1980

The miser thinks not as the free,
Nor cunning as simplicity.

Nid unfryd ynfyd a chall,
Nid unfryd cybydd a chorodyn.

1981

Roguery, through fear of shame,
Will come in cleverness's name.

Tan enw pwyll y daw twyll.

1982

No worship has he
Who a lacquey can be.

Nid ymweis a fo parch.

1983

The tongue alone
May break a bone.

Tafawd a dyr asgwrn.

1984

No earnest paid,
No bargain made.

Nib newid heb fach.

1985–6–7–8

None the fox in stealth exceedeth,
None the dog in faithful care ;
Tricks no ape a-teaching needeth :
What so shifty as the hare ?

Nid dichellgar ond llwynawg ;
Nid cywir ond ci ;
Nid cyfrwys ond epa ;
Nid ystrywgar ond ysgyfarnog.

1989–90–1–2

A sheep the model is of meekness ;
Hens for ever waste and spoil ;
Nought can match a mole for sleekness ;
Nought so foul as is a boil.

Nid rhadlawn ond dafad ;
Nid afradlon ond iar ;
Nid esmwyth ond pathew ;
Nid brwnt ond ffwlbert.

1993

Short-lived were servants if their fare
Were but the poultry which they share.

Rhan y gwas o gig yr iar.

1994

With a natural impulse flows
The bounty which a father shows.

Rhan gorwydd o dad.

1995

Your stomach and back
Your riches will rack ;
What either may spare,
T' other asks for its share.

Rhannu rhwng y bol a'r cefn.

1996

The poorest, fleeing, has a suite
As a nobleman's complete.

Rhieddawg anghenawg ar ffo.

1997

When on your bounty comes a call,
Large be your gift, your promise small.

Rhodd fawr ac addaw bychan.

1998

The hen that next the cock doth stand
Will never swerve on either hand.

Ni wyr yr iar nesaf i'r ceiliog.

1999

'Tis early, giving in July
Directions for your Christmas pie.

Son am Awst wyliau 'r Nadolig.

2000

One slow to move
Will awkward prove.

Swrth pob diawg.

2001

He did the deed who lays the blame ;
Shepherd and wolf are oft the same.

Sef yw blaidd y bugail.

2002

'Tis not by his own body that
A gnat gives being to a gnat.

Nid o'i gorph ydd ymre y gwybedyn.

2003

The sergeant that discovery made
Of a lost ox, when it had strayed,
From thigh of that found ox's hide
With ankle boots shall be supplied.

Y rhingyll a ddyly goesau yr ychain ac y gwartheg a gaffer o'i
gyhudd ef, i wneuthiur cranau cyfuwch a'i uffarnau.

2004

From the source of the fountain,
From the ocean's far end,
From the heart of the mountain,
God blessing can send
To the good, and the bad
Who his badness will mend.

O for, ac o fynydd,
Ac o waelod afonydd,
Y denfyn Duw dda i ddedwydd.

2005

Cold is the juice that you will drain
From the reeking battle plain.

Oer yw isgell y galanas.

2006

Of every fluid you may hold
That its natural state is cold.

Oer pob gwlyb.

2007

Many a brave word will let fall
The man behind a castle wall.

Gair gwr o gastell.

2008

The thief is a more dangerous guest
Than he who lies where you should rest.

Gwell cynnwys got na lleidr.

2009

Fierce are mastiffs ; hounds sagacious ;
      Dark and secret is the bat ;
Fell the lion and voracious ;
      Ever venomous the cat.

Nid ffyrnig ond ci ;
Nid ethrylithgar ond ystlym ;
Nid gwenwynig ond cath ;
Nid creulon ond llew.

2010

Leap but to show
How roebucks go,
And you will show, upon the spot,
What the roebuck's leap is not.

O mynni nodi y iwrch, ti a fwri naid amgen.

2011

To the place where you did churn,
For buttermilk you may return.

Pa le yn y ffuddai y mae yr enwyn.

2012

Agile coolness be your hope
When a fierce dog sweeps the slope.

Rhuthr ci o gribarth.

2013

Safe lies the mallet which we push
Within a bristling holly bush.

Khoi 'r ordd dan y celynllwyn.

2014

If on two stools a man will sit,
Ere long his limbs the floor will hit.

Rhwng y ddwy ystôl ydd â'r din i lawr.

2015

A bull's whole prowess lies before ;
His haunches speed the battling boar.

Nerth tarw yn ei dwyfron ;
Nerth twrch yn ei aflach.

2016

They who long all they see to touch
Will have an eye that sees too much.

Rhy-foddawg rhy fawr a wyl.

2017

Withered to grey, and worn to bare,
The field is where men hold a fair.

Llwyd yw 'r farchnad.

2018

Of believing
Comes deceiving.

Twyll drwy ymddiried.

2019

The longer treaties reading take,
The shorter is the peace they make.

Hir ammod nid â i dda.

2020

Poor creature ! Ever on the run,
Yet nothing for himself has won !

Gwae, a drô o glun i glun,
Ac ni feddo beth ei hun.

2021

Better with money make away,
Than hoard and covet night and day.

Gwell corrawg na chybydd.

2022

The moment when the cat departs
Gives back to mice their merry hearts.

Llawen fydd y llygoden prŷd ni bo'r gath gartref.

2023

The Sunday were of little boot
On which we might not stir a foot.

Rhag bod y sul heb siglaw.

2024

Lest some ill hap the hawks befall,
When falconers make festival,
Three cups of purling mead be all
That falconer may drink in hall.
But, not to stint him of his fare,
In courtly vessels, sweet and rare,
For soberer hours be kept his share.

Nid yf yr hebogydd namyn tri chornaid yn y neuadd, rhag bod gwall ar ei hebogau drwy fedd-dawd : llestri hagen erfyll ei wirawd yn y llys.—*Laws.*

2025

The knowledge that is still to earn
Be it thy lesson still to learn.

Oni byddi cyfarwydd cyfarch.

2026

A burthen no stout man refuses
Is the coracle he uses ;
But let him coracle beware
Whose burthen he can lightly bear.

Llwyth gwr ei gorwg.

2027

Poor soul, that hungry watch maintains
Upon a sheepskin after rains.

Gwae a arhoo ei giniaw
O din dafad wedi gwlaw.

2028

Argument is out of season
When with wolf a deer doth reason.

Mal yr hydd a'r blaidd.

2029

Words from the lip, as from the bow
Arrows, irrevocable go.

Mal y saeth o'r llinyn.

2030

Goodness is hired, but not by pelf ;
For each good action pays itself.

Yn mhob daioni y mae gobrwy.

2031

The glutton, when he says his grace,
Forgets the blotches on his face.

Ni ddaw cof i lwth ei grach.

2032

No man his dues
Through me shall lose.

Ni ddaliaf ddilys o ddyn.

2033

The plough, as it goes,
Will wipe its own nose.

Sychu trwyn y swch.

2034

The ship that bears a wooden freight
Will never founder with its weight.

Ysgafnlwyth a glûd coed.

2035

By penury the stubborn pay
For having gotten their own way.

Nid ysgar anghenawg ac anhyfryd.

2036

Rome's building was a work not done
Between sunrise and set of sun.

Nid yn undydd yr adeilwyd Rhufain.

2037

The name of wise he never loses
Who utterance to his thought refuses.

Doeth pob tawgar.

2038

What God hath will'd
Shall be fulfill'd.

A fynno Duw derfydd.

2039

The man who like a reed can shake,
A trembling reed will tremble make.

Nugiaw gan y cawn.

2040

Adulterers will always share
The load of hate that thieves must bear.

Nid gwell got na lleidr.

2041

Thrice her wanton cup would fill
The woman of a wanton will.

Teirgwers gwraig rewydd.

2042

With cart in front, and horse behind,
Your wares their market never find.

Rhoi 'r car o flaen y march.

2043

Speed some penalty and pain
After every oath profane.

Telitor gwedi halawglw.

2044

What a single hound hath taken,
Soon by all the pack is shaken.

Nugiaw gan y cwn.

2045

Of punishment the cat makes fun
Whom you turn out into the sun.

Troi 'r gath yn yr haul.

2046

When two for ever would contend,
A bet will controversy end.

Terfyn cywiraf cyngwystl.

2047

A great toll own'd, and taken all,
Will bring you in a toll that's small.

Toll fawr a wna toll fechan.

2048

So long as harrows going be,
Thorn hurdles you will going see.

Tra retto'r ôg, y rhêd y ddraen-glwyd.

2049

Strong though your will and efforts are,
Still stronger is your ruling star.

Trêch tynged nog arfaeth.

2050

He on a salary would thrive
Whom honour cannot keep alive.
Triccid wrth barch ni thrig wrth ei gyfarws.

2051

Him never spurn
Who'll serve thy turn.
Abl i bawb a'i gweinyddo.

2052

Vainly ever shall we blame
Hunger's triumph over shame.
Rhag newyn nid oes gwyledd.

2053

The strongest vassal wielding sword
Is weaker than the pettiest lord.
Trêch gwan arglwydd nâ chadarn wâs.

2054

If for a patron you've a mind,
To curse and railing be resign'd.
A garo ei gilydd nid adnebydd ei gabl.

2055

Never success with any side
By God disfavour'd will abide.
Tu, ni fynno Duw, ni lwydd.

2056

If an adult'ress woman be,
It so was writ in Fate's decree.
Tyngedfen gwraig ot.

2057

'Tis law that all the kindred pay,
Whene'er their kinsman man shall slay,
A fine which, as we daily hear,
Is called 'The penny of the spear.'
But such a name each woman shields
Who for a spear the distaff wields.

Ceiniawg baladr yw yr hon, a dalai bob gwr o'r genedl tu ac at
dalu galanas : ni thal gwraig baladr, am nad oes iddi ond cogel.

Laws.

2058

Unnoticed still the stomach lies
Until its voice in craving rise.

Tywyll boly hyd pan lefair.

2059

In a land where none can see,
The one-eyed man a king will be.

Unllygeidiawg fydd brenin yn ngwlad y deillion.

2060

Breathing of late the prison's breeze
You'll be the better for a sneeze.

Untrew o garchar.

2061

What can more insidious be
Than the suasion of a fee ?

Twyllwr yw gwobr.

2062

With all your heed and all your skill,
Misfortune may supplant you still.

Trychni ni hawdd ei ochel.

2063

No man so fit thy mate to be
As he who is compeer with thee.

Abl i bawb ei gydradd.

2064

If enough to delight,
Enough it is quite.

Abl i bawb a'i boddlono.

2065

In places three
God most will be :
Where loved, where sought
Where self is nought.

Tri lle y bydd y mwyaf, ynddo o Dduw : lle mwyaf bo a'i cais ;
y mwyaf a'i car ; a lleiaf o hunan.

2066

As near to speechless brute doth come
The ever-silent, as the dumb.

Aflafar yw tawedawg.

2067

Who loveth me,
My dog love he.

A'm caro, cared fy nghi.

2068

It must be expected
That the mourner be dejected.

Trist pob galarus.

2069

As old birds caw or crow, 'tis law
With the young birds to crow or caw.

A gre y frân fawr a gre y frân fechan.

2070

He who once his seat doth leave,
Hardly will his seat retrieve.

A gyfodes a golles ei le.

2071

The timorous must
For aye mistrust.

Anhyderus pob ofnawg.

2072

Lords pocket what to give you choose.
Lords take what you to give refuse.

Arglwydd a gymhell.

2073

The yoke which ties a man to sin
Is the spirit that's within.

Amaerwy direidi drwg anian.

2074

Fair and gladsome o'er the earth
Shines the bonfire for a birth.

Teg tân bob tymp.

2075

Muscle and nerve the wound sustain :
Death drives victorious through the vein.

Anaf yn ngiau, angeu yn gwythi.

2076

He with whom life no more can stay
Tell me not dies before his day.

Angheu angen dyhewyn dir.

2077

The cross-bred soul
Takes no control.

Anhydyn pob afrywiawg.

2078

The hall where patience keeps her school
Of knowledge is the vestibule.

Amaerwy adnabod ammynedd.

2079

The dog as fierce a watch will hold
O'er bag of salt as bag of gold.

Amgeledd y ci am y cŵd halen.

2080

If a husband's wedded wife
On his concubine, in strife,
Unarm'd, with two fierce hands shall make
Such onset as her life to take,
There is no law that shall requite
The kin of her who law did slight.

Hwrdd gwraig wriawg yn ei chywres a'i dwylaw oni gyfarfoent,
cyd bo marw ni ddiwygir.—*Laws.*

2081

No dignity the rude attain
But what is sallow in the grain.

Anwar fu felyn ei fraint.

2082

Detraction deal,
Detraction feel.

A ogano a ogenir.

2083

He is polluting God's estate
Who doth a man contaminate.

A lygrwys Duw, a lygrwys dyn.

2084

What is buck, and what is doe,
The glutton's appetite will show.

Arwydd nad cig bwch.

2085

A sliver from the osier bed
Will neatly crown grimalkin's head.

Asglodyn gwern y'mhen y gath.

2086

To him who goods hath, goods are given
And with him thrive as he hath thriven.

Lle byddo da y rhoir ac y tycia.

2087

The thing by God's own judgment done,
Man will pronounce his judgment on.

A wnel Duw dyn a'i barn.

2088

Or broad or long, in either case
An inch is still an inch of space.

Cystal modfedd o lêd a modfedd o hyd.

2089

From distance high
Pride casts her eye.

Balchder o bell.

2090

Be happy and gay
Thy natural way.

Bid anian dedwydd.

2091

Those bargaining best understand
Who the best bargain make for land.

Goreu cyfnewid cyfnewid o dir.

2092

The stream that in its channel flows
Is still at home where'er it goes.

Cyfarwydd dwfr yn ei ddyfrlle.

2093

A title he to good hath won
Who to another good hath done.

A wnel mâd mad a ddyly.

2094

Planted are your spearmen well
In the gorges of a dell.

Bid reiniad yn nghyfarth.

2095

With brain in an eddy,
The man is unsteady.

Y bendro wibwrn.

2096

These chaces three,
Of nine that be,
With shout and cry of hound you'll scare
The pheasant, weasel, and the bear.

O'r naw helwriaeth tair helfa gyfarthfa sydd : arth, dringiedydd,
a cheiliawg coed.—*Laws.*

2097

Let be, though wearisome, the strain
Of the sick bemoaning pain.

Bid nych cwyn clâf.

2098

High always is the bullock's worth
When reckoned ere the calf has birth.

Budd cyn tymp.

2099

Fools speak without
Reserve or doubt.

Blaengar ymadrawdd ffol.

2100

Of Bardic life the blended source
Is light with harmony and force.

Tri chyntefigion beirdd ynys Prydain : Plenydd, alawn, a Gwron.

2101

Tones must to words of right belong :
No singing is there but of song.

Canu heb gywydd.

2102

As a word never spoken
Is the word that is broken.

Addewid, nis gwneler, nid yw.

2103

Cowards, while fear their blood doth curdle,
Will shake and quiver like sea girdle.

Crynu mal y forwialen.

2104

Ask not his mother, would you know
If Taffy be a thief or no.

Gofyn i mam a wyf fi leidr.

2105

With the lip
We can but sip

Bychodedd minialedd.

2106

On the best errand is he bent
Who with the crucifix is sent.

Gorcu neges myned a chroes.

2107

That as confession Justice takes
Which unenforced the culprit makes

Cyffes pawb rhwydd.

2108

Every amorous glance you see,
As scornful in a trice can be.

Golwg serchawg syberw fydd.

2109

God, whatever colt He see,
Knows that colt a colt must be

Ebawl yr ebawl i Dduw.

2110

Good is he who bore the brunt
Firmly, scathless, and in front.

Da yw a saif ac ni, waner.

2111

Every man his choice may make
What of his own meal to take.

Dewis pawb o'i giniaw.

2112

More hath he than *quantum suff.*
Who of figs has ate enough.

Digon yw digon o ffigys.

2113

If that one be bad, the rest
Find you will not of the best.

Drwg un drwg arall.

2114

Enter thy house for good or ill,
And happen let what happen will.

Dala dy dŷ am a fo a diofryd a ddarfo.

2115

To things their proper terms apply,
If you description make your care ;
Your words by apt connection tie,
And like unto its like compare.

Tri pheth a bair iawn ddyfalu : iawn ddewis ar air ; iawn ieithyddu :
ac iawn gyfelybu.

2116

He who doth a surety proffer,
Nothing owns which he can offer.

Dyly mach ni ddyly ddim.

2117

All have their luck, but the unfortunate
Meet with good fortune when it is too late.

Hwyr waith i anffynnedig.

2118

Beneath a stormy April's sky
The pig is littered but to die.

Ebrill garw,
Porchell marw.

2119

Whene'er a footmark you can trace,
A hand has visited the place.

Elid llaw gan droed.

2120

Little will a promise bring
Between two women chattering.

Eddewid gwragedd deueiriawg.

2121

Though named, he has a nameless state
Whose name can never carry weight.

Enw heb senw.

2122

Loathsome creature must be he
Who by none beloved can be.

Ffiaidd ni charer.

2123

Badly as any nights be passed,
We leave a worse night for our last.

Gadu y nós waethaf yn olaf.

2124

Upon the good man's barn he preys
Who to the spoiler it betrays.

Gollwng drygwr i ysgubor gwrda.

2125

Wisest counsel will be given
By the man who best hath thriven.

Gnawd cysyl dedwydd yn ddoeth.

2126

The father was enriched by fraud ;
The child roams penniless abroad.

Gnawd difrawd ar blant enwir.

2127

Buffet and shake
Clowns give and take.

Gormes y taiawg ar ei gilydd.

2128

He who on down found no repose
Sleeps deeply in the church at Rhose.

Hir hun Maelgwn yn eglwys Rhos.

2129

Swift comes, as sudden 'twas to go,
What comes sent forth from a crossbow.

Gnawd buan o fras.

2130

The dog that takes to run away
Runs worse and wilder every day.

Gwaeth-waeth rhed y cwn.

2131

The noblest fast is that you make
When money you forbear to take.

Goreu newyn yr ariant.

2132

Nothing on earth about doth face
With the returning furrow's grace.

Goreu gwrthwyneb gwrthwyneb cwys.

2133

Insolent the words which fall
From the lips of Pleasure's thrall.

Gnawd o ben drythyll traha.

2134

What by slightness enter'd in,
For departure should be thin.

Ysgawn i mewn, ysgawn i maes.

2135

The fool a finger always tries
To have within his neighbours' pies.

Pob ffol a fyn ymyrraeth.
Cas a ymyrro ar bobpeth heb achaws.

2136

Of fortune he will be the sport
Who loses favour in a court.

Gwae ddigariad llŷs.

2137

No thought can ever be expected
Except from mind on self reflected.

Nid myfyriaeth ond ystyriaeth.

2138

All the eyes of lovers all
Will on their beloved fall.

Golwg pawb ar a garo

2139

Though with thy stake transfix'd, yet will
The Severn be the Severn still.

Gwan dy bawl yn Hafren, Hafren fydd hi fal cynt.

2140-1-2-3

Many a game can Britain brag.
First comes 'Put badger into bag.'
Next, of sheer strength a trial true,
'I am the best man of the two.'
'The old dog playing with the pup,'
And 'Green the wound is,' four make up.

Gwarai broch y' nghod ;
Gwareu 'mi trech ; '
Gware 'hengi a cholwyn ; '
Gware 'gweli ir.'

2144

The thing thy neighbour left with thee,
Hopeless his pledge again to see,
Just when it seems thine own, and seems
Invaluable,—he redeems.

Gwartheg arall yn adnau, pan fo chwegaf, ni fydd tau.

2145

With his ear, as with his eye,
Will the vigilant descry.

Gweled ei glust â 'i lygad.

2146

Stronger will two old women be
Than any one, though strongest she.

Gwell nerth dwywrach nag un.

2147

If once the fires of Hell were out,
Heaven would be little cared about.

Ychydig a wneid am y nef, pei diffoddid uffern.

2148

From the merit which achieveth
Gold, its lustre gold receiveth.

Gwiw aur i a 'i dirper.

2149

Press we a child to go or stay,
To either his reply is 'Nay.'

Gŵr fab
Ti a gai nâg.

2150

Old women have been known to die
Even on the slope of Mabon high.

Gwrach a fydd marw etto yn Rhiw Fabon.

2151

The traitor who his lord betrays;
    The thief five pennies' worth who thieves;
The man who man in malice slays:
    These three no fine from death retrieves.

Tri dyn y sydd eneidfaddeu ac ni ellir eu prynu : bradwr
arglwydd ; a dyn a ladd arall yn ffyrnig ; a lleidr cyfaddef am
werth mwy no phedair ceiniawg.—*Laws.*

2152

Of Charity he gives a proof
Who gives the shelter of a root.

Goreu cardawd rhoi lletty.

2153

Enough at court a little stay
To make you wish yourself away.

Gwrthlys i bawb llys a fydd.

2154

Pow'rless would be hell flame to burn
Him who gave good for evil turn.

Gwna dda dros ddrwg,
Uffern ni 'th ddwg.

2155

When you at sea let fly a crow
You'll hardly bid him landward go.

Gyru brân i geisio tir.

2156

All that so mean
Can say ' fifteen.'

Hawdd yw dywedyd pymtheg.

2157

Longer than long that pain doth cling
Which nothing to an end can bring.

Hir gnif, nid esgor ludded.

2158

Or win respect
Or bear neglect.

Ni chymero ei barch cymered ei anmharch.

2159

If to the January sky
The niggard sun his face deny,
The next two months their powers combine,
And make him with a vengeance shine.

Haul yn Ionawr
Ni mâd welawr,
Mawrth a Chwefrawr
A 'i dialawr.

2160

If one who suffers debt's distress,
As many as three coats possess,
To pay his dues, the laws decree
That he shall part with two of three.

Can ni bo ddyledur namyn tri thuddedyn, efe a ddyly dalu yddau.

Laws.

2161

Tiresome the state
Of all who wait.

Hir pob aros.

2162

Wasps that never honey make
None the less to honey take.

Cylion a dynant at y mel.

2163

Better cross to others be
Than have Fortune cross to thee.

Gwell rhy raws na rhy ruan.

2164

Take but one footstep short and slow,
The three that follow will be so.

Un cam diogi a wna ddau a thri.

2165
One word that warns of ill before
Out-values two that ill deplore.

Gwell un gair ymlaen, na dau yn ol.

2166
People oft drive the dog away
Whom they could not persuade to stay.

Gyrru y cŷn, a gerddo.

2167
To the queen's handmaid ne'er refused
Be—land, enfranchised all,
All garments by the queen disused,
And palfrey at her call.

Llawforwyn y frenines ei thir a gaiff yn rhydd : hi a ddyly ei
march preswyl, a hen ddillad y frenines.—*Laws*.

2168
If one will wrangle from a wood,
His reasons may be understood ;
But one within a castle wall
His reasons may for ever bawl.

Haws dadleu o goed nog o gastell.

2169
The smallest bite of bitter food
Seems always long in being chew'd.

Hir y cnoir tammaid chwerw.

2170
Better one friend in need to see
It is, than to have sent for three.

Gwell un cynnhorthwy na dau wŷs.

2171

Milk but little, and that, too,
Buttermilk to taste and view.

Ychydig laeth, a hynny yn enwyn.

2172

Drops falling soft, but falling still
For years, the marble rock will drill.

Y dafn a dyll y gareg, nid o gryfder, ond o fynych syrthio.

2173

Dry will water be, fire be wet,
Before a silent wife you get.

Tri pheth anhawdd ei cael: dwfr sych ; tan gwlyb ; a gwraig dawgar.

2174

Bounty, when ruined by expense,
Turns to penurious indigence.

Hael pob colledig anghenawg.

2175

By his fruit
The man soon showeth
The kind of root
From which he groweth.

Ysbys y dengys y dyn,
O ba radd y bo 'i wreiddyn.

2176

This oft of simpletons the case is :
Rogues eat their meals before their faces.

Ysu bwyd yr ynfyd yn y blaen.

2177

Better a single finger clasp
Than the whole fist have in your grasp.

Ys gwell cau a bys, nag a dwrn.

2178

Evil, be sure,
Is evil's cure.

Drwg ys dir rhag drwg arall.

2179

Your daughter more to draw is able
Than can draw your strongest cable.

Gwell y tyn merch nâ rhaff.

2180

Of dogs thee'd rather hang than keep
Men lightly say that they kill sheep.

Y ci, a fynner ei grogi, a ddywedir ei fod yn lladd defaid.

2181

If one by poison other slay,
Two penalties that fiend shall pay :
His felon life is forfeit made ;
A fine upon his kin is laid ;
And in the king's breast doth it lie
Whether by fire or rope he die.

Y dyn a laddo arall â gwenwyn, galanas deuddyblyg a dâl, canys
ffyrnig yw : a bid enaidfaddau am y naill, a'r llall ar ei genedl, a'i
ddyhenydd fydd yn ewyllys yr arglwydd, ai ei losgi ai ei grogi
a fyno.—*Laws.*

2182

The way in which a giver giveth,
With his gift for ever liveth.

Ystum llawgar yn rhannu.

2183

Highest cunning art is nearing
When as simplicity appearing.

Celfyddyd gyfan rwydded ei deall nis gellir cynnefinach o'r symledd.

2184

In every form which things can take
Death too will its appearance make.

Ynmhob rhith y daw angeu.

2185

On him at mill who answers call
The last of the belated all,
Let hard vindictive labour fall.

Y diweddaf a orddiwedder ar y freuan, ar hwnnw y dielir.

2186

Others their trouble need to spare,
The listless trouble need, and care.

Rhaid i segur beth i'w wneuthur.

2187

No recompense will come so slow
As that behaviour must bestow.

Hwyra' tâl tal ymddwyn.

2188

With all warfare
Goes anxious care.

Ynmhob rhyfel y mae gofal.

2189

Sigh, maiden, for some loving soul ;
Sigh, beldam, for the caudle-bowl.

Uchenaid gwrâch ar ol ei huwd.

2190

With ears, eyes, claws, and tail complete ;
Rat-killing ; free from scar of fire ;
Good mother ; rare in monthly heat :
Such is the cat which you require.

Teithi cath yw, bod yn gyfglust, gyflygad gyfewin, gyflosgwrn difan o dan, a lladd llygod, ac na chathderica bob lloer, ac nag yso ei chwenawon.—*Laws.*

2191

The matter well is writ which, when received,
Is apprehended, relished, and believed.

Tair cainc hyweddiant iaith ; a ddeelir ; a hoffir ; ac a gredir.

2192

One hand that with a fire doth play,
In wool a hundred hands will lay.

Un llaw ar 'i dân, canllaw ar 'i wlan.

2193

Sick sheep that bleat, sick kine that low,
Give token that to death they go.

Trengis, a frefwys.

2194

Better the child by 'mother' led
Than the child on mother fed.

Gwell 'moes law' na 'moes fam.'

2195

To countries strange strange manners leave,
And to thy native manners cleave.

Pob gwlad yn ei harfer.

2196

Seed must you spill
Where reap you will.

Oni heir ni fedir.

2197

A filthy man, if saint he be,
Will for his filth more honour'd be.

Perchi gwr er ei fawed.

2198

He shows but a fastidious care
Who won't say 'horse' of any mare ;
And he to language uses force
Who will say 'mare' of any horse..

Onid march ys caseg.

2199

Bold thief, to pledge the silver bowl
With him from whom his plate he stole.

Adneu gan berchen.

2200

Make up by sleight
Your lack of might.

Oni byddi grŷf bydd gyfrwys.

2201

Whoever makes fourteen his price
About fifteen will not be nice.

O down ni er pedwar ar ddeg
Ni a ddown er pymtheg.

2202

Pars, cui sexus inest, partem, cui sexus inhæret,
Sola adeat ; solâ sola fruatur eâ.

Elid rhyw a barth pa yw.

2203

If we're to go,
Then be it so.

O down ni
Ni a ddown.

2204

The stranger wreck'd on Britain's shore
Whate'er he plunders shall restore ;
But till three days and nights are o'er,
No punishment shall suffer more.
For strangers into crime will draw
Their ignorance of speech and law.

Dynion anghyfieithus a fwrier o long i dir, hyd yn mhen tair nos a
thridiau, yn i wyddant cyfraith y wlad, ni ddylyir arnynt am eu
lledrad amgen nog edryd i'r colledig yr eiddaw.

2205

If there be a chance it may,
The chances are the other way.

Odid nad odid yw.

2206

Strong is a dog in tooth and jaw ;
Give me a bear for arm and paw.

Nerth ci yn ei ddaint,
Nerth arth yn ei freichiau.

2207

With a sparrow nought can vie
For an amorous gallantry.

Nid anllad, ond aderyn y to.

2208

Charity to all the same is,
Heedless where the praise or blame is.

Nid ystyr cariad cywilydd.

2209

Love ne'er to human being went,
Preceded by disparagement.

Nid oedd hôff car ni ddifenwyd.

2210

No ruling sense
Like Providence.

Nid llywiawdr namyn Duw.

2211

That play may not be sport, they feel
Who play with iron, fire, or steel.

Nid chwareu chwareu a thân, nac â dûr, nac a haiarn.

2212

No treaty ever such ally
As is a brother will supply ;
And auxiliary none
Will such be as your brother's son.

Nid cyweithas ond brawd.
Nid diwyd heb nai.

2213

Never may an alien's word
Against a Briton's voice be heard.

Nid gair gair alltud ar Cymro.

2214

Would you have music from a rook,
You first must teach it him by book.

Nid cynnefin brân a chanu.

2215

Forget the priest does, soon and quite,
The days when he was acolyte.

Nid cof gan offeiriad ei fod yn glochydd.

2216

'Tis hard to get upon its road
That which is neither truss nor load.

Nid bwrn, nid baich.

2217

Quite a rarity now
Is a farmer at plough.

Odid a ardd.

2218

Never to rack and ruin went
The things which I had never lent.

Nid benthyg ni hanfo gwaeth.

2219

Too dull man's sight is, and too short.
To see whence cometh his support.

Nid wyl dyn, a'i pyrth.

2220

Bleddyn barks fiercely ; but his bite
Will help to cure you of your fright.

Nid cymmaint Bleddyn a'i drwst.

2221

Decorate with star of wood
The man you hold for little good.

Ni rown erddo seren bren.

2222

God's own work is far too true
For God ever to undo.

Nid adwna Duw a wnaeth.

2223

No mouse will ever think it best
In the cat's tail to lay her nest.

Ni wna y llygoden ei nyth yn llosgwrn y gâth.

2224

Good which in his dad's house he could not see,
In his wife's father's house adoreth he.

Ni weles da yn nhŷ ei dâd a hoffes da yn nhŷ ei chwegrwn.

2225

The wrong of wrong cohabitation
Is not redress'd by compensation.

Ni thal dim drwg ymread.

2226

If falling tree a man shall slay,
The woodsman for his blood must pay.

O derfydd i ddyn ladd pren, a dygwydd o'r pren a lladd dyn taled
werth gwaed.—*Laws.*

2227

I draw not from another's toe
Thorns, that they into mine may go.

Ni thynnaf ddraen o droed arall, a'i dodi i 'm troed fy hun.

2228

His country's justice cannot seek
The man who will or can not speak.

Ni roddir gwlad i fud.

2229

Never did Arthur storm the fort
Which was a woman's last resort.

Ni thorres Arthur nawdd gwraig.

2230

No knowledge lies in human brains
Complete as that the book contains.

Ni wyr yn llwyr namyn llyfr.

2231

If to a lord rough tongue you show,
   A fine upon your head is set ;
Slander a mean man ever so,
   Fineless and harmless off you get.

Ni thelir gweli tafawd namyn i arglwydd.

2232

Fat meat will on no board appear
Through all the months of every year.

Ni phery cig bras yn wastad.

2233

The beggar, whom you drive away,
Behind the nearest bush will stay.

Ni phella yr ehegr neb tylawd.

2234

Nearest neighbour cannot know
Nearest neighbour's pain or woe.

Nid wyr dyn dolur y llall.

2235

More never in one crossbow case
Than one crossbow will find a place.

Ni eing deufras yn unsach.

2236

The ox that's black from hoof to head
Upon your foot will never tread.

Ni sengis yr ych du ar dy droed.

2237

The cat of which I hope to brag,
I do not purchase in a bag.

Ni phrynaf gath yn ffetan.

2238

He who did never stumble make
Shall never prosperous journey take.

Ni llwydda ond a dramgwydda.

2239

Heart a-going ;
Breath a-blowing ;
Thought a-flowing :
In these repose
Man never knows.

Tri pheth ydynt yn gorphwys un amser mewn dyn : y galon yn
gweithiau, ac yr eneid yn meddwl.

2240

Sighs but too often pass the throat
For that which is not worth a groat.

Nid uchenaid rhag gwael.

2241

Three persons your obeisance claim :
A chief, a stranger, and a dame.

Tri holiadolion addwynder : pennaeth ; benyw ; a dyeithr
cymmrawd.

2242

The gifts which fall to beggars are
Not presents sent them from afar.

Ni phell anrhegir tlawd.

2243

Its name of judgment ill hath got
Judgment from one who hearken'd not.

Ni eill barnu ni wrandawo.

2244

To him who food amiss did take
His stomach owes a stomach ache.

Ni ddyly drygfoly namyn drwgysu.

2245

What councils hatch
Still needs despatch.

Ni dderfydd cynghor.

2246

Dearly you must buy, or steal
Cleverly, a labourer's meal.

Ni cheir bwyd taiawg yn rhad.

2247

No pippins you'll see
Upon a crab tree.

Ni cheir afal pêr ar bren sûr.

2248

Not until he lost his store
Did ever Welshman lock his door.

Ni cheidw Cymro oni gollo.

2249

Ne'er will come
All from some.

Ni ellir cwbl o anghwbl.

2250

He who is starved, and long has been,
Will not be loved if he be seen.

Ni cherir newynawg.

2251

Attain the good he only will
Who is impatient of the ill.

Ni cheiff dda ni ddioddefo drwg.

2252

A money bag is all he takes
Who prize of an old woman makes.

Ni cheffir mwy na chod gan y wrach.

2253

God's love despair
Will never share.

Ni char Dofydd diobaith.

2254

With many a bosom thought is mixt
The aurelia on the bosom fixt.

Meithrin chwileryn ym mynwes.

2255

Not ever abide
Will Easter tide.

Ni bydd preswyl Pasg.

2256

In sober truth, you never can
Show me a good-for-nothing man.

Ni bydd gwr wrth ddim.

2257

No license have we to be smart,
Until we play in the first fool's part.

Ni bydd cymhen neb, oni fo ynfyd cysefin.

2258

Deliver'd ere the sun doth rise
Attack is doubled by surprise.

Gnotaf cyrch gan fore.

2259

Arthur never was but when
He was seen to be by men.

Ni fu Arthur ond tra bu.

2260

See will you never in your life
A fair neck in a scoundrel's wife.

Nid mynyglwen gwraig drygwr.

2261

No honour attends
One who never makes friends.

Ni chaiff rhy anfoddawg rhybarch

2262

Like fire that's kindled on a hearth,
Spring flowers up in congenial earth.

Mal y tân yn yr aelwyd.

2263

He bears him as no man of straw
Who in a castle gives the law.

Mawreddig pendefig castell.

2264

The ill-conditioned never saw
A year without a suit at law.

Ni bydd diriaid heb hawl.

2265

Officious as officious may be
Is an ape about her baby.

Mal yr ab am ei cheneu.

2266

Never has horse been killed outright
By journeying a single night.

Nid marw march er unnos.

2267

If fishes for the water long,
Their need, as their desire, is strong.

Mal y pysg am y dwfr.

2268

The man was never very wise
Who ne'er on letters turned his eyes.

Ni bydd doeth ni ddarlleno.

2269

She who doth perfect beauty own
Wears, like a naked flower full-blown,
No jewel but herself alone.

Mal y peithiant ymdeg.

2270

A hog will find, though no one teaches,
The short way to a grove of beeches.

Mal y moch am y ffawydd

2271

No escape can be so narrow
As would a frog's beneath a harrow.

Mal y llyffan dan yr og.

2272

The man is as good
As the neighbourhood.

Mal y cant, y gwr.

2273

Little from little takes it all:
Mill ponds are puddles when they fall.

Mal llyn melin ar drai.

2274

The man who well and truly serves
Will hold the place that he deserves.

Gwâs da a gaiff ei le.

2275

His labour skilful was and stout
Whose dam still keeps the water out.

Gorug ei waith a fach y fachdaith.

2276

The natural gift you'll never see
Until by art it lesson'd be.

Lle, ni bo dỳsg, ni bydd dawn.

2277

With one hand can a woman take,
And with the other present make,
While with her headpiece she doth mind :
A proper woman there you find.

Gweddus ar wraig, y naill law yn casglu, y llall yn rhannu, ac ei phen yn pryderu.

2278

Your wain looks handsomest, be sure,
When it is loaded with manure.

Llawer càr baw ymdeg.

2279

Bounding over ice, the stone
Sings a song that's all its own.

Llais maen yn oerddwfr.

2280

A crown whose jewels out are torn
A head is that's eyeless made, or born.

Mal llygad ym mhen.

2281

Affectation all eschew ;
As thy foot is, be thy shoe.

Lladd y gwadn fel y bo'r troed.

2282

To the needy
Trust is all
Which their own
They still can call.

Hoff gan anghenawg ei goelio.

2283

Happiness is never true
To man his whole existence through.

Oed y dyn ni chanlyn y da.

2284

Colt many days
A pony stays.

Hir y bydd march bach yn ebol.

2285

Where now he is, there long will be
An infant in a hollow tree.

Hir yw'r mab yn y ceubren.

2286

Each ridge of ploughman's perfect art
Is of a mile the thousandth part.

Mil o ryniau a wna filltir.

2287

Of all the teeth the heaviest fine
Meets damage done to the canine;
For of all teeth, on either hand,
As guards in either jaw they stand.

Gwerth pob un o'r ysgythredd dwy fuw a deugaint ariant ; canys
bugel y dannedd ynt.—*Laws.*

2288

Many will to the feast repair
Who have no invitation there.

Gnawd osb er nas gwahoddir.

2289

Care not to give denial strong
To deeds which law exempts from wrong.

Nid rhaid gwad dros orsaf.

2290

The message will a wolf prefer
That's sent through his own messenger.

Diwytaf i fleiddian ei genad ei hunan.

2291

Not an ox, but a hide,
Is an ox that hath died.

Cnu y ddafad farw.

2292

Deprecate the use of fists ;
To heels let take whoever lists.

Eiriach law, nag eiriach droed.

2293-4

For his lord's life an outlaw be
The man who from the law did flee.
For him the land shall not receive
Who land and law did basely leave.

Os adaw y llys a wna dyn yn anghyfreithiawl ei ddyfarnu a uneir
yn oes ei arglwydd breuffo ye orsedd hono, can ni einyn mro ni
roddo wir.—*Laws.*

2295

Oftenest and most
Fail brag and boast.

Llawer mawrair a fethla.

2296

Love for her husband will inspire
The wife to love her husband's sire.

A garo ei gwr cared ei chwegrwn.

2297

That horse the best is that I know,
Which takes me when and where I'd go.

Goreu march un a'm dyco.

2298

A little with a blessing graced
Surpasses much that runs to waste.

Gwell ychydig yn rhad no llawer yn afrad.

2299

' A druid,' so a druid spake,
' It is impossible to make.'

Nid ellir derwydd, medd derwydd.

2300

Pleasant sally, quick retort,
Are language to befit a court ;
Voices that conflict and call
Make the hubbub of a brawl.

Siarad yn brestl, siarad yn ddestl.
Siarad yn westl, siarad annestl.

2301

When the worst arriveth here,
Then the better draweth near.

Dyddaw drwg, hanfyddir gwell.

2302

Complain he should not of unrest
Who keeps a beetle in his breast.

Magu chwil yn mynwes.

2303

None of the royal vests disused
Are to the chamberlain refused,
Save those in which the monarch went
To chill and gall his flesh in Lent.

Gwas ystafell biau hen ddillad y brenin oll eithr ei dudded grawys.

2304

But once to hell a journey make
They who to hell their passage take.

Nid eir i annwfn ond unwaith.

2305

As is the garment that we wear,
So God appoints us cold to bear.

Duw a ran yr annwyd fal y rhan y dillad.

2306

Of having help then surest you make
When of yourself good care you take.

Adnes yw ymgeledd.

2307

For fairness, nothing we call fair
With even justice can compare.

Namyn iawnder ni enwir aes.

2308
'Tis a wise action foolish made
To close the fold whose sheep have strayed.
Cau y drws wedi myned y defaid allan.

2309
Into the world, each living thing,
Some female body forth must bring.
Pob byw o aig a ysgar.

2310
Never yet did mirth and care
At once a single bosom share.
Handid efrddwl aflawen.

2311
What seems unlikeliest to speed,
Will, better than the best, succeed.
Annhebyg biau ffyniaw.

2312
Perjury's sin they do not share,
Who, for what good is, ill forswear.
Nid anudon ymchwelyd ar y da.

2313
Give doubt alone
To things unknown.
Ammhau pob anwybod.

2314
If obedient, kind, and just,
Worship God aright you must.
Addoli Duw yw bod yn gyfiawn, yn ufudd ac yn drugarawg.

z

2315

If a woman's two feet,
As her tongue is, were fleet,
To kindle her match,
She could lightning catch.

Pei cygynted ar draed ag ar dafawd y bydda wraig, hi a ddalai
ddigon o luched i gynneu tan y bore.

2316

One woman can, what cannot do
A hundred thousand men for you.

Can mil wraig.

2317

A fever, or a fright, can make
A giant like an aspen shake.

Cryn fal dail yr aethwydd.

2318

A suit of armour he bestows
Who warns of peril, which he knows.

Arfawg a gaffo rybydd.

2319

'Tis pitiful false oath to take,
And get no credence for its sake.

Cas a ddyngo lw anudon, ac ni bo neb yn ei gredu.

2320

Higher, as nobler of descent,
Is that, which is an element,
In being and in quality,
Than ought, that's composite, can be.

Goruwch o ran bonedd yw y peth, a saif ar under hanfod ac
ansawdd ar bob cymhleth hanfod ac ansawdd.—*Bardic.*

2321

Once incur we Fortune's spite,
Nothing ever will go right.

Anhappus pob trwch.

2322

Few are the scholars, rare the school,
Where well is taught 'Indulge and rule.'

Gormes esmwythder fydd anhawdd ei drin.

2323

Highest is lowest after fall ;
And chief of men, no man at all.

A fu bencwd, aeth yn dincwd ; a fu dyn, aeth yn adyn.

2324

When a noble ; vex'd with life,
Sends for death to end the strife ;
Thou wilt do his errand best,
Thou, of men the laziest.

Wyd burion i gyrchu angeu at wr boneddig.

2325

Best in that neighbourhood you'll dwell
Where all the neighbours love you well.

Lle da i bawb lle y carer.

2326

Of three things one a guest will balk,
And make his feast no feast at all :
An edgeless knife ; a broken fork ;
And all the dainties out of call.

Tri pheth anharddwch i wr mewn gwledd : pwyniad ryfer, cyllell
finbwl, ac y saig yn mhell.

2327

One sure defect which Envy shows, is
The want of sense, which it discloses.

Nid pwyllig y dyn, a ddalio genfigen.

2328

Not toil, but grace, brings toil its fruit ;
But God with grace the toil will suit.

Dedwydd, Dofydd a'i rhydd rhad.

2329

Ponder thy word
Before it is heard.

Rhagreithia dy air cyn noi ddodi.

2330

A keeper's assistant, or strapper of groom,
By little pretension will greatly presume.

Gwas i ragwas, *neu*, gwas i was y cwn.

2331

When these three things inform the mind,
Wisdom is not far behind :
Lore, in moral laws acquired ;
Love of toil by toil inspired ;
A soul with native genius fired.

Tri rhagweinyddiaid doethineb: addysg ddeddfawl; arfer weithred-
awl ; a serch awenawl.—*Bardic.*

2332

Meat in sight, and hope of meat,
Brings a pipkin set to heat.

Bwystlawn callawr.

2333

Through the gates of Death we see
What a better world will be.

Trwy byrth angeu y cawn olwg ar fyd sydd well.

2334

If necessity impose it,
Let us take, as if we chose, it.

Troi rhaid yn rheswm.

2335

True lord and owner is, you'll say,
Not he with whom his own doth stay,
But he who owns to give away.

Yda nid eiddo 'r cybydd
Yr hael a'i rho pieufydd.

2336

May the right hand never shake
From which the needy bounties take.

Na chryned llaw a rano i reidus.

2337

Man gives, what good a body needs,
And God with good the spirit feeds.

Dyn a ran da yn ei raid,
Duw a ran da i'r enaid.

2338

No beast through Wales so ravenous stalks
As that two-legged beast who talks.

Rheibusaf un yn holl wlad Gymmru,
Yw'r un deudroediawg a wyr lefaru.

2339

Some are there, who would strip the skin
From off the man, who lives within.

Rhathu y croen oddiar gefn, a'i dyco.

2340

Then Slander's sword is fatal made,
When seeming truth hath edged the blade.

Blaenu cledd athrawd a rhith gwirionedd.

2341

Rush onward with resistless might
Do they, whom Want impels in flight.

Rheidiawg achenawg ar ffo.

2342

Fated to fall
Leaders are all.

Diwedd pob rhwyf rhewintor.

2343

Hateful is to every ear
The voice, that doth a parent jeer.

Cas anmharchu rhiant.

2344

You will not say, 'The desert stayed me,'
When a field of wheat waylaid thee.

Nid diffeithwch gwenith, a luddio ffordd rhodiadur.

2345

If a stranger ask advice,
Answer true, and in a trice.

Rhaid rhoi deall i alltud.

2346

'Twixt 'give' and 'take' the difference clear
Is a hundred pounds a year.

Can punt yn y flwyddyn yw gwahaniaeth rhwng 'dos' a 'dyre.'

2347

For three things thankful voice we lift :
A bidding ; warning ; and a gift.

Tri pheth a ddyly pawb ei ddiolch : gwahawdd ; rhybudd ; ac
anrheg.

2348

A secret loathing we conceal
When sued for love, we cannot feel.

Ffiaidd, ni charer.

2349

No man quite naturally whistles,
While he naked goes through thistles.

Ni ehofn noeth yn ysgall.

2350

In each land that is known,
Hath a seed been self-sown,
From which office hath grown.

Had swyddogaeth a dyfant yn mhob tir.

2351

With a smile you will hear
From the spiteful his jeer.

Chweirys gwawd o anianawd .

2352
Cross-grain'd is every he and she
With blemish or deformity.

Astrus pob anaf.

2353
You'll walk as easy, and as quick,
As you will ride upon a stick.

Cystal ar draed a marchogaeth ar ffon.

2354
Bards ever are we
For purposes three :
Manners to mend ;
Peace to befriend ;
Excellence all in good works, to commend.

Tair dyben barddoniaeth : gwellâu moes a defawd ; cynnal
heddwch ; a moli pob daionus a rhagor.—*Bardic.*

2355
Needless is it to add more
When you've said ' The man's a bore.'

Cas fydd a oreillitio.

2356
To being taught the aids are three :
Sense ; feeling ; opportunity.

Tri pheth a gynnull addysg : synwyr ; syniad ; a dichwain.

2357
The wash-girl's refuge is a ring
Wide as her beetle she can fling.

Golchuries, ei nawdd yw hyd y gallo fwrw ei golchbren.

2358

It is late for taking thought,
When the trap has sprung and caught.

Mae yn hwyr difaru yn ol i'r ffagl gynnu.

2359

Custom will school
To obey and to rule.

Arfer a wna meistri.

2360

He who with the best would vie,
Topmost in the sack to lie,
Deeds must to himself forbid,
That at bottom would be hid.

A fyno bod yn bencwd, na wnaed a wedd i dincwd.

2361

Just when you please, dry gorse you'll fire ;
Not quench it, just when you desire.

Hawdd tanio eithin crinion ; nid hawdd eu diffawdd.

2362

Thy love unto thy neighbour yield :
But not thy weapon, nor thy shield.

Car dy gymydawg, ond na ro iddo na 'th gledd na 'th darian.

2363

The leech, the warrior, and the tike,
Their greatness owe to blood alike.

Tri pheth mawr o ymchwydd ymborth ar waed : gele ; horen ;
a rhyfelwr.

2364

Man will knowledge get and save,
From his cradle to his grave.

Ef a geiff dyn ddysgo 'i febyd hyd ei henaint.

2365

A heavy heart
Bids health depart.

Afiach pob trwmgalon.

2366

The primal Unities are three,
Which three and one must ever be :
One God ; one truth ; one central peace,
Where balanced oppositions cease.

Tri un cyntefig y sydd, ac nis gellir amgen nog un a thri honynt :
un Duw ; un gwirionedd ; ac un pwnc rhyddyd, sef y bydd lle
bo cydbwys pob gwrth.—*Bardic.*

2367

Discreet is a mind
To silence inclined.

Doeth pob tawgar.

2368

While all things else shall shift and roam
Truth ever truth is, and at home.

Gwir tros byth yn yr unman.

2369

There will be the narrowest strait
Where widest things approximate.

Ing yn ing yngon eangedd.

2370

Wholesome it is hot bread to smell
Unless you eat it hot, as well.

Iachus arogli bara twym, afiâchus ei fwyta.

2371

A plot against yourself you weave
Whene'er another you deceive.

Twyllaw arall twyllaw yth hunan.
Twyllaw arall yn fawr twyllaw yth hunan yn fwy.

2372

Warm as cat by fire of coal
Is a dormouse at the pole.

Cydwymed a'r pathew.

2373

Blood in veins is sooner hot,
Than is water in the pot.

Cynt y twyma gwaed no dwfr.

2374

The lover of his bliss restrains,
    A short night of incessant wet ;
Or restless door, whose hinge complains ;
    Or scold, that can no slumber get.

Tri anhyborth serchawg : nos fer wlawiawg ; dor wichiedig ; a
gwraig anhunawg ymgeingar.

2375

All the peace that we know
To our weapon we owe.

Arf a geidw heddwch.

2376

Conscience is the nest to brood
All the vital germs of good.

Cydwybod yw y nyth, lle ydd ymddëor pob daioni.

2377

'Tis an abominable thing
    To make one's pride what shame should bring.

Cas a ymffrostio o'i gywilydd ei hun.

2378

Corn, milk, and herbs are healthful cheer ;
Will lengthen life ; the mind will clear.

Tri ymborth dyn a barant iechyd, hiroes, a synwyr gloew ; ydfwyd ;
blithfwyd ; a garddfwyd.

2379

Of all the bad, an idler deem
To be in worthlessness supreme.

Nid mall dryfall ond diogi.

2380

Noble rank, which we inherit,
Is a rank that men bestow ;
Noble rank, achieved by merit,
Is a rank to God we owe.

Bonedd ynnill bonedd o Dduw :
Bonedd geni bonedd o ddyn.

2381

Better in pillory to stand
Than shake the informer by the hand.

Gwell pren cyhuddiad no dyn cyhuddgar.

2382

What innocence hath said in jest
Guilt turns to sober truth expressed.

Euawg a dry y cellwair yn wir.

2383

Of a brave man the heart
Is his weapon's best part.

Arf glew yn ei galon.

2384

Of all men most provoking he
Who must always meddling be.

Cas a ymyrro heb achaws.

2385

On Earth we roam,
With Heaven for home.

Nid tref
Ond nef.

2386

The load, that starts a scanty load,
Gets, often, bulky on its road.

Ysgafn lwyth a glud.

2387

If minstrel, smith, and bard they be,
Three men will make society.

Tri dyn a wnant cyfanedd lle bont : bardd ; gof ; a thelyniawn.

2388

Strength needs he, tact, and patience too,
Who trails a hook the forest through.

Mal tynu bach trwy goed.

2389

Signs you will see
Of Genius three :
Fancies fine, and
Fancies changing ;
Fancies never
Lawless ranging.

Tair cynneddf awen : hardd feddwl ; priodawl feddwl ; ac amry-
wedd feddwl.

2390

A splendid cup that holds no wine ;
Big barn that keeps no corn ;
Such is a woman fair, and fine,
Of reputation shorn.

Tri pheth tebyg y naill i'r llail : ysgubawr deg heb yd ; mail
deg heb ddiawd ; a merch deg heb ei geirda.

2391

As likely kill a friend as foe
They who at a venture throw.

Ergyd ar gais.

2392

Three things to do words should not fail :
Arouse ; describe ; and tell a tale.

Tair swydd iaith : adrawdd, cynhyrfu, a dyfalu.—*Bardic.*

2393

Dainties purveyor ne'er supplied,
Such as a greyhound will provide.

Nid asborth ond milgi.

2394

Each man owns, by all opinion,
O'er his own a lord's dominion.

Arglwydd pawb ar ei eiddo.

2395

Tho' a life so protracted may be
That more than five score years its stay be,
Some one day and night
Will finish it quite.

Yr hoedl, er hyd fo'i haros
A dderfydd yn nydd a nos.

2396

Mercy's work you need not stay
On the holiest holiday.

Nid oes gwyl rhag Elusen.

2397

Those cast in lawsuits law will blame :
The neediest are first to claim.

Tost yd gwyn pob colledig,
Ffest yd hawl eisiwedig.

2398

A foolish king
A fearful thing.

Cas brenin heb doethineb.

2399

Gaily at thy country railing
Charge her with no shameful failing.

Cellwair dy wal, call air da,
Uwch y wledd, na chywilyddia.

2400

While cure on cure the old woman makes
Her own head miserably aches.

Ni weryd y gwrach ei phen.

2401

Those, who of life have taken leave
Our longing never will retrieve.

Hiraeth am farw ni weryd.

2402

With a woman often blamed
Goes a woman unashamed.

Bid wastad gwraig o'i mynych warth.

2403

Odious as a servant he
Who without a fear shall be.

Cas gwasaneuthnyn heb ofn.

2404

We play at bowls
With Saxon polls.

A gware pelre a phen Saeson.

2405

He, who, from want or love of pelf,
Maintains no servant to attend him,
Nor wills, nor skills, to serve himself,
Is pitiful, till heaven mend him.

Cas ni bo ganddo a 'i gwasaneutha, ac ni's gwasaneutho ei hun.

2406

For him, who loves the yoke 'tis fit,
To love as well the bows of it.

A garo yr iau,
Cared ei waryau.

2407

Satan two hands hath on him cast,
And given him a fall at last.

Mae diawl wedi cael gwall arno.

2408

Of those who felony abet,
The first black mark on him be set
Who told with tongue dyed red in blood
The murd'rer where his victim stood.

Cyntaf o naw affaith galanas yw tafod ruddiaeth : mynegi y neb a
ladder, i'r neb a'i lladdo.

2409

He needs no screen
Whose hands are clean.

Llaw lan diogel ei pherchen.

2410

Wales could the babe-like Mona smother,
Yet Mona is of Wales the mother.

Mon mam Gymmru.

2411

Years tell on all things as they're told ;
Man's memory only grows not old.

Ni hena ceudawd.

2412

No man knoweth how to muse
Until for love his heart he lose ;
And no one loveth through and through
Unless he love the Muses too.

Nid meddylgar ond serchawg ; nid serchawg ond cerddgar.

2413

The more we struggle and debate,
The more distressful is our fate.

Po mwyaf y drafod mwyaf fydd y gorfod.

2414

Of womanhood the virtues three
Are : in her wishes kind to be ;
Of manners gentle and sedate ;
In loving, only, passionate.

Prif ragoriaeth merch yw gwarineb, a mwynder, a serch.

2415

Let but the lion leave his throne
Some fox will make the seat his own.

O eisiau llew ydd â llwynawg i'r orsedd.

2416

For these is growing
All our knowing :
Profit ; beauty ;
And our duty.

Tri dyben gwybodaeth : dyled, budd, a phrydferthwch.

2417

Restlessness itself must be
What is as restless as the sea.

Mor ansefydlawg a'r mor.

2418

Your voices to the height you'll raise
When it is concord that you praise.

Nid moliannus ond cyundeb.

2419

Men hope from battle life to save,
None hope for rescue from a grave.

Mae gobaith gwr o ryfel, nid gobaith neb o'r bedd.

2420

God in the men takes no delight
Who of these three things love the sight :
Parade ; a monster ; and a fight.

Tri pheth y sydd, ni char Duw a'u caro : gweled ymladd ; gweled anghenedl ; a gweled rhodres balchder.

2421

The giant Rhys a mantle made
With beards of kings, whom he had flay'd.

Rhita gawr a wnai bilys o grwyn barfau breninoedd.

2422

From earth springs up no pillar'd gold
The roof of bad men to uphold.

Pan nad rhyfedd na thyf post aur drwy nen ty yr enwir.

2423

A boggy way,
An endless day.

Hirddydd, merydd mae.

2424

Silence of patience is the fruit ;
And thought of patience is the root.

Nid tawedawg ond goddefus : nid goddefus ond synwyrawl.

2425

The man who lets not man direct him
Waits for misfortune to correct him.

Nis myn pwyllad.

2426

Exempted from the axe's stroke
Are your birch tree, witch elm, and oak,
Until to fell them you receive
Your feudal lord's and country's leave.

Tri phren nid rhydd eu torri, heb gennad gwlad ac arglwydd :
mesbren, sef derwen ; bedwen ; a rhafnwydden.—*Laws.*

2427

Less easy 'tis to satisfy
A feaster's stomach than his eye.

Haws llenwi bol no llygad.

2428

Skin whole and with no bones that ache
'Twere wonder if he lay awake.

Hawdd cysgu mewn croen cyfan.

2429

The cry, with which a kindred cries,
Will ascend into the skies.

Gair teulu yn esgyn.

2430

To sing aright, unto thy song
See that three qualities belong :
Be the measure smooth and true ;
Be description like the view ;
With noble spirit all imbue.

Tri rhagoriaeth canu : iawn fydryddu ; iawn ddyfalu ; ac iawn
ymddwyn.

2431

Fortune all states doth make to feel
These changes of her rolling wheel :
The wealth of peace will war beget ;
War be with poverty beset ;
To peace again turn want and debt.

Gwiliwch y droell,
A fo cryf a fag rhyfel ;
Rhyfel a fag rhyw afar
Tlodi, byth at lid a bar ;
Tylodi, trueni trwch
A fo caeth, a fag heddwch.

2432

His gift remembers many a day
The man who rarely gives away.

Hir ei gof ni mynych rydd.

2433

None in their terms will sooner meet
Than will the greedy and the cheat.

Hawdd tangnefedd rhwng twyll a thrachwant.

2434

To tell how feasts and seasons fall
Free is astronomy to all :
And fate by stars to prophesy
None worse or better know than I.

Ni chain sywedydd yn unfron.

2435

Dull weather wet, dry weather gay,
Justly each other's work repay.

Y gwlaw a'r hinon a dalant yn gywir y naill i'r llall.

2436

True maid's true dress
Is bashfulness.

Gwisg oreu merch yw gwylder.

2437

To show herself a cow complete,
A cow each ninth of May should greet
With milk through every teat a-flowing,
And calf nine paces after going.

Nawfed dydd Mai y dyly buwch fod yn deithiawl ; dawed laeth
o ben pob teth iddi, ac ymdaith o'i llo naw cam yn ei hol.

2438

To Arthur's court right only brings
Professors, and the sons of kings.

I neuadd Arthur, namyn mab brenin gwlad teithiawg, neu
gerddawr a ddyco ei gerdd, ni ater i mewn.

2439

Every man by God is taught
To set its limit to his thought.

Meddwl dyn
Duw a'i terfyn.

2440

Relics of things to ruin gone
In the universe live on.

A aeth ynghyd
A aeth i'r byd.

2441

Man well on three things thought bestows,
Whence is he? Where? and, Whither goes?

Tri pheth a ddyly dyn ei ystyried, o ba le y daeth, yn mha le
y mae, ac i ba le yr el.

2442

Lore from three fountains fills her urn :
Thought, Fancy, and the power to learn.

Tair ffynnon gwybodaeth : crebwyll, ystyriaeth, a dysgeidiaeth.

2443

When Saxons Irishwomen wed,
    No ceremony more they make,
Before they enter marriage bed,
    Than o'er a besom jump to take.

Priodas Sais a Gwyddeles neidiaw dros ysgubell.

2444
More by hard cleaning silver may
Than by hard use be worn away.

Dywinaw yr arian yn ddim.

2445
While placemen grow in every ground
Where can the man for place be found?

Had dysteiniad a dyfant yn mhob tir, had synwyr braidd y tyfant
yn un tir.

2446
Between the little hand and sleeve
Enough, enough you may perceive
Of her, who is your heart's desire,
Your brain to melt, your blood to fire.

Gennid rhybuched rhwng llaw a llawes.

2447
The best he thrives
Who owns beehives.

Goreu llwyddiant gwenyn.

2448
Something beyond the bridge will be
Though nothing but the bridge you see.

Nid pont heb draphont.

2449
The law I never will apply,
Where on the man I can rely.

Ni ddaliaf ddilys o ddyn.

2450
If both your eyes on aught you throw,
A name on it you can bestow,
And so describe that all shall know.

Nid rhaid ond bwrw trem ar un peth o'r byd ac yna yn gyflawn ei
nodliwiaw a'i hanesu.

2451

What to the glutton's stomach goes
The miser in his cupboard stows.

A grawn cybydd a ys glwth.

2452

For man's first sin a stern decree
From Eden drove the honey bee;
But as from paradise he went,
God to the bee his blessing sent.

Bonedd gwenyn o baradwys pan yw; ac o achaws pechawd
dyn y daethynt oddyno ac y dodes Duw rad arnynt.

2453

No traveller can to and fro,
The world through, like a penny, go.

Nid trwyddedawg ond dinair.

2454

Often laughing to excess
Is a trick of wantonness.

Gnawd gan rewydd rychwerthin.

2455

The fine for blood, by kindred paid,
Is on no childless woman laid.

Ni thal gwraig anfab alanas.—*Laws.*

2456

Lost is his sight
To awkward wight.

Dall pob anghyfarwydd.

2457

To work their best let others roam,
The lone one's work must guard his home.

Goreu gwaith undyn gwarchadw y ty.

2458

The villain's hand itself will sever
From the villain's self for ever.

Llaw ddiriaid a ddydawl ei pherchen.

2459

By child of God three signs abide :
He takes not in his virtues pride ;
Void is his conscience of offence ;
And patience is his self-defence.

Tri nodau plant Duw : ymddwyn difalch ; cydwybod lan : a
dyoddef camwedd yn amyneddgar.

2460

A graceful fool
Is not the rule.

Anghymmen pob ffol.

2461

The malicious, for his labour,
Gets the luck he wished his neighbour.

A fyno ddrwg i'w gymydog iddo ei hun y daw.

2462

The reindeer is born
To be strong in his horn.

Nerth algar yn ei gorn.

2463

The odds are double
That want brings trouble.

Nid esgar anghenawg ag anhyfryd.

2464

None of the plainest can have been
The sight that in the dusk was seen.

Nid eglur edrych yn nhywyll.

2465

Three things man's rudimental state
Irremovably await :
His breach of laws ; his doom to die ;
Escape through death, and bliss thereby.

Tri chynghyd anhebgor abred : anghyfraith gan nas gellir
amgen ; dianc angeu rhag drwg a chythraul, a chynnydd bywyd
a daioni.

2466

A false oath slips
Through filthy lips.

Aflan genau anudonawl.

2467

Never except on chicken's food
Of chickens will you rear a brood.

Ni bydd byw cyw heb aliw.

2468

Hornets stinging ; oxen tearing :
The teamsman's patience out is wearing.

Rhwng y clyr a thin y gwartheg.

2469

To customs, down from old that flow,
The laws themselves precedence owe,
But customs from a doubtful source
O'er least and weakest have not force.

Cynnefawd a ragflaena gyfraith eisoes o ddamwain anniau ac yna
ni chymmell hi neb.

2470

Her marriage portion shall retrieve
The wife that does her husband leave,
Because her soul he did aggrieve
By a habit cold and faint,
By a scrofulous complaint,
Or a breath that hath a taint.

O dri achaws ni chyll gwraig ei hegweddi, cyd adawo ei gwr, o glafri, ac o eisieu cyd ac o ddryganadl.

2471

Of bears a baying hunt we make
For when their flesh we will,
Dogs soon the savoury wretch o'ertake,
And bark, and bait, and kill.

Yr arth yw helfa gyfarthfa am ei bod yn gig hely o'r pennaf, ac am na bydd fawr ymlid arni am nasgall gerdded, ond yn araf; ac ni bydd ond ei baeddu, a'i chyfarth, a'i lladd.—*Laws.*

2472

God scourge the false one twice believ'd
And God scourge me, if thrice deceiv'd.

Anffawd i ddyn a'm twyllodd ddwywaith : anffawd i minnau o'm twyllo y drydedd waith.

2473

' Yes ' confesses
Silence ' Yes ' is.

Addef yw tewi.

2474

More the imprudent seldom gain
Than poverty, mishap, and pain.

Tri pheth a geiff dyn annedwydd ; tlodi, ac aflwyddiant, a phoen.

2475

Good enow
It was for sow.

Abl yw soeg i foch.

2476

The leaf that rustles in the wind
Brings home its guilt to guilty mind.

Llais dalen yn y gwynt
A darf gydwybod euawg.

2477

An heir, if at fourteen he lose
His sire, shall his own guardian choose.

Yn bedwar ar ddeg y caiff etifedd ddewis ei arffedawg.

2478

Of country life the quiet ceases
When your plough is all in pieces,
When your homestead is in flames,
When your land a lawyer claims.

Tri arludd tir, hawl yn nadlau, neu dor aradr, neu losgi ty ar y tir.

2479

Bring us Time, what bring it may,
It ne'er will bring us yesterday.

Ni ddaw doe byth.

2480

Two points in three a sow hath got,
That as a sow befit her,
If much to boar she runneth not,
Nor e'er devour her litter.

Teithi hwch yw, na bo baeddredawg, ac nad yso ei pherchyll.—

Laws.

2481

Quick is the eye of him to see
Who comes for hospitality.

Craff fydd llygad y gwestwr.

2482

Well kept, a string of flaxen twine
Will turn into a silken line.

Cadw dy lin, ef a â yn eurllin.

2483

As from a sleep, which off I shake,
Out of error I awake.

Ac yna mi a ddeffroais.

2484

A man that loves the forest well
Of every tree the growth can tell ;
Its bole, its branches, and its root,
Its bud, its blossom, and its fruit.

Am bren dyfaler ei dwf teg, ei faint, a'i frig, a tharddiad ei flagur a'i
falant, a'i flodau, a'i ffrwyth.

2485

Whenever surety given be,
   All in one band
   Must be the hand
Of debtor, creditor, and bail :
   For if of three
   But one be free,
Slip will the suretyship and fail.

Oni bydd y tair llaw wrth roddi mach, balawg fechni y gelwir. —

Laws.

2486

To foul, to hunt, and catch the carp,
Recite the Welsh, and play the harp ;
Of song in four parts, part to take ;
To blazon arms, and verses make ;
To ride as envoy of the nation :
Are a boy-Briton's recreation.

Deg mabolgamp y sydd : hely a milgi ; hely pysg ; hely aderyn :
barddoniaeth ; canu telyn ; darllain Cymraeg ; canu cywydd
pedwar ac acenu ; tynu arfau, herodraeth.

2487

It was not kindness that he meant you
When he on such an errand sent you.

Nid a'th garwys a'th anfonwys yma.

2488

A judge be made no man alive
Until his years be twenty-five ;
For not till then can beard be grown
And none is man till beard he own ;
Nor seemly is 't that youth presume
On aged heads to pass its doom.

Yr oed y dylyir gwneuthur dyn yn yngnad yw ei bum mlwydd ar
ugaint, sef, achaws yw wrth na bydd barf arno hyd yna ; ac na
bydd gwr nebun hyd pan ddel barf arno ; ac nad teg gweled
gwas ieuanc yn barnu ar wr oediawg.

2489

A cat grown old,
And thin, and cold,
In life will abide,
Whatever betide.

Cath annwydawg hen
Bo a fo arni, byw fydd.

2490

Where promise ready is, and great,
Performance will be small and late.

Addaw mawr a rhodd fechan.

2491

As fee to chamberlain be paid
The cushion underneath him laid.

Y gwas ystafell a geiff y gobenydd a ddoter dano yn ei gader.

2492

The king's door-keeper the king's way
Must clear with truncheon as he may,
And the law none, whom he shall smite,
Within arm's length, will e'er requite.

Y drysawr a ddyly rwyddâu ffordd i'r brenin a'i ferllysg, a pha ddyn
bynnag a darawo i ar y ffordd o hyd ei fraich a'i ferllysg, cyd
gofyno iawn iddo ni ddyly ei gaffael.

2493

The song trips gaily from the tongue
That hath a license to be sung.

Gwell cerdd o'i breiniaw.

2494

When onions fail,
Put up with kail.

Oni cheffi gennin dwg fresych.

2495

He who with sieve for water goes
Will waste his water on his toes.

Myned a gogr i'r afon.

2496

If beast attack and kill a beast,
With which its nature bids it fight,
From claim its owner is released
The damaged owner to requite :
But if 'tis nature's wont for each,
With other peacefully to stay,
The aggressor's owner, for the breach
Of nature's law must damage pay.

Ni thal un anifel brwydrin eu gilydd : sef yw y rhai hyny ; amws
ni thal y llall ; na tharw y llall ; na buch eu gilydd : na baedd y
llall ; na hwrdd ei gilydd ; na cheiliawg y llall ; ac o'r lladdant
hwy anifeiliaid ereill hwynt a'u talant.—*Laws*.

2497

Give me a buck,
For making muck.

Nid tomlyd ond bwch.

2498

Do not for a paltry price
Part with anything that's nice ;
Nor, merely for its being small,
Part with anything at all.

Na werth er bychodedd.

2499

Let ploughman hand to driver lend,
The stiff ox yoke to bend ;
The driver's hand will be enow
To loose the ox from plough.

Yr amaeth a ddyly gymhorth y geilwad o ddaly yr ychain ; ac ni
ddyly ollwng namyn y ddau fyrieuwys.—*Laws*.

2500

Praise, what is good, as praise you may ;
Of what is evil, nothing say.

Canmawl dda ; taw ddrwg.

2501

To make a lawful flock of sheep,
Thirty, and a ram, you keep ;
To make a lawful herd of swine,
With a boar sows three and nine.

Maint cadw cyfraith o'r moch, deuddeg llwdn a baedd ; maint
cadw cyfraith o'r defaid, deg llwdn ar ugaint a hwrdd.

2502

Your slave, for whom no price was paid,
Who willingly to serve you stayed,
Has twice the value of the slave
For whom the highest price you gave.

Caeth dofaeth yw dyn a drico o ganiad heb ei brynu gyda mab
uchelwr ; a gwerth hwnnw yw dau cymaint a gwerth caeth a
bryner.

2503

Genius will its owner render
Loving, generous, and tender.

Tair effaith awen : haelioni ; gwarineb ; a charedigrwydd.

2504

Each summer and each winter tide,
To the head groom an ox's hide,
Bridles to make, shall be supplied,
For horses that the king doth ride.

Y pengwastrawd a gaiff groen ych y gauaf, a chroen ych yr haf, i
wneuthur cebystrau i feirch y brenin.—*Laws.*

2505

By hundreds borne, not kept by any,
Such is the nature of a penny.

Yr un geiniawg a addug gant.

B B

2506

Small honour to the cook will come,
Who, cooking, never licks his thumb.

Mefl i'r cog, ar ni lyfo ei law.

2507

If one a chattel warrants, he
Answers for its security ;
But not against a tyrant lord ;
And not against a robber horde ;
And not against a thievish hand ;
Nor an invader's martial band :
And if thus lost till 'tis regain'd,
The suretyship is not maintain'd.

Cyfraith a ddywed, na ddyly mach gynnal cyfechni y peth y bo
mach arno, rhag trais, nag rhag lledrad, nag rhag anghyfarch,
nag rhag ysbail yni ddel peth hwnw drachefn yn llaw y neb y
cychwnid i ganto.—*Laws.*

2508

Of disrespect he makes him sure
Who is slovenly and poor.

Cas tlawd a wrthod grynodeb.

2509

'Tis fickle heart, or empty pate,
That without cause deserts his mate.

Cas a adawes ei gydymmaith heb achaws.

2510

Whene'er the timid wades, the sea
Up to his waist will never be.

Ni ad mor hyd ei wregys.

2511

Inhabited is every land
Where goes the plough, and buildings stand.

Adail ac aradwy yw cyfannedd.—*Laws.*

2512

Elements four the body's whole,
And forces three compose the soul.

Y corff a gyfansoddir o'r pedwar defnydd, a'r enaid a gyfansoddir
o'r tri nerth.—*Bardic.*

2513

Within three spheres our life is ranging ;
Free choice ; and suffering ; and changing :
And what these latter two will be,
The first forbids us to foresee.

Tri angen-orfod dyn : dioddef ; newid ; a dewis : a chan allu
dewis ni wyper am y ddau arall cyn digwydd.—*Bardic.*

2514

Each wise-woman's charm
Increases the harm.

Cyfareddion gwrach waeth waeth.

2515

If by misfortune or neglect,
    One bound to find the king his meal,
Fail : to no power, that will protect,
    Or make excuse, can he appeal.
But if one well the king receive,
    Of every royal servant there
Line must he with a coin the sleeve,
    His barns to save, his stacks to spare.

Nid oes nawdd rhag y brenin i'w gwynosawg ; y neb a ddylyed
ei borthi y nos hono, ac ni's portho.   Cwynosawg brenin a ddyly
roddi ceiniawg i'r gwasanaethwyr er arbed ei yd, a'i ysgubawr.

B B 2

2516

Pincers, sledge-hammer, punch and bore,
In value each are pennies four,
And four times is the anvil more.

Gefail, gordd, cethrawl, tryorydd pedair ceiniawg cyfraith a dal
pob un ; y cwnsyllt, cymaint a dal ag y pedwar hynny.

2517

A faultless he or faultless she,
Go where you will, you'll never see.

Nid oes neb heb ei fai.

2518

Outrages to all must be
Waylaying, blow, or robbery.

Tair fordd y sarêir pob dyn yn y byd : o daraw, a gosawd,
a dwyn trais arno.—*Laws.*

2519

Long last, and closely will cohere,
A friendship made by peer with peer.

Addas i bawb ei gydradd.

2520

He keeps with ease his reckoning true
Who counts but up to number two.

Ni golles ei gyfrif a ddechreuis.

2521

He by his bees will never thrive
Who eats his honey from his hive.

Bwyta y mel o'r cwch.

2522
No drain of pity will you win
From the fiend who shar'd your sin.
Cynghraiff diawl cynghwl cywyd.

2523-4
If one's kinsman's life be taken,
Occasions three our vengeance waken :
    When the women wail and cry ;
    When his bier is passing by ;
    When the grave mound meets our eye,
Where he lies murder'd and forsaken.
Tri chyffraw dial y sydd : diaspedain caresau ; gweled elawr eu
car ; a gweled bedd eu car heb ymddifwyn.

2525
You never will see
Good and bad to agree.
Ni chynfydd diriaid a da.

2526
Snatch'd will by others be his share
Who on division is not there.
Ni weler, dyger ei ran.

2527
Not he that's prettiest to the view,
But he that manliest deeds can do.
Gwell dynoliaeth da no drych.

2528
On a long journey set your mind,
When you a generous soul would find.
Hir hynt a chyrchu llawgar.

2529

While watchmen on the ramparts sleep,
God o'er his city ward will keep.

Pan gysgo pawb ar gylched, ni chwsg Duw pan rydd gwared.

2530

As the richest rich is he
Who covets nothing he can see.

Y cyfoethaf, y neb ni chwennycho ddim ar gam o eiddaw ereill.

2531

A good-for-nothing woman she
To whom all men are company.

Ni thâl dim, gwraig a gymdeithioco â phob gwr.

2532

Of pride is telling,
The bosom swelling.

Gnawd bronrain balch.

2533

No hindrance he, nor danger knows,
Who rings his adversary's nose.

Dodi trwyll yn ei drwyn.

2534

The wise his rage
Will soon assuage.

Ni bydd doeth yn hir mewn llid.

2535

Where you see resemblance striking,
There you'll find a mutual liking.

Pawb a gar ei gywala.

2536
Two crafts the accomplish'd hand will ply—
To bring relief, or give supply.

Dau waith a fydd gan gywraint.

2537
The horse you see, of canvas made,
Is of an unseen man the shade.

Nid oedd efe ond march cynfas i'r llall.

2538
The oath for a head huntsman's lips
Is, By my hounds, my horn, and slips.

Pan dyngo y pencynydd, tynged i fwyn ei gwn, a'i gyrn, a'i gyn-
llyfanau.

2539
Customs that with the law contend
Make mischief till they make an end.

Cynnefawd a lygro gyfraith, ni ddylyir ei chynnal.

2540
He, who threatens, breathes but breath,
He, who strikes, may deal a death.

Nid ergyd ni gywirer.

2541
In the realm where bliss doth reign,
We first from three things freedom gain :
Penury, and death, and pain.

Tri chyntefigaeth gwynfyd : annrwg, aneisiau, ac annarfod

2542
If glance on me dark beauty throws,
That darkness is the dawn of woes.

Nid yw ond dechreu'r drwg
Rhwng Gwen liw'r mwg a minnau.

2543

What's won upon the war steed's back,
Beneath his belly goes to rack.

A gasgler ar farch malen dan ei dôr ydd â.

2544

Would you a man's secret take,
You will best your capture make,
If you ask him by surprise ;
Or your manner blind his eyes ;
Or your questions seem so distant,
That he stints not his replies.

Tair ffordd sydd i chwiliaw calon dyn : sef yn y peth nas tybio,
yn y modd nas tybio, ac ar y pryd nas tybio.

2545

Changeful ever you will find
Moon, and wind,
And woman's mind.

Tri pheth a newidiant yn fynych : y lleuad, y gwynt, a meddwl
gwraig.—*Laws.*

2546

That deed unto thyself forbid
Thou in another wouldst have chid ;
That action of thyself require
Thou from another wouldst desire.

Tair deddf gweithredoedd dyn : a waharddo yn arall, a geisio yn
arall, ac ni waeth ganddo ba wedd y bo gan arall.—*Bardic.*

2547

His instinct will take
The stag to the lake.

Addug yr hydd i'r llyn.

2548

His message must the porter bring
Upon his knees unto the king.

Ni ddyly y drysawr eistedd yn y neuadd, namyn ar dal ei ddeulin
gwneuthur ei neges wrth y brenin.—*Laws.*

2549

Where the river doth roll
With a noise, it is shoal.

Basaf dwr pan yd lefain.

2550

Though speck in size, in savour faint,
One grain of dirt the cheese will taint.

Mae baw yn y caws.

2551

The tongue, that pleasant things will say,
Through the wide world can make its way.

Tafawd teg a â trwy y byd.

2552

To know a miser is to know
The miser's friend to be his foe.

Gelyn gan gerlyn ei gar.

2553–4

These three prerogatives doth God enjoy:
To make new out of old, yet nought destroy,
To bear the stress of Time's eternal range,
And be all changeful forms, yet never change.

Tri pheth nis gall namyn Duw : dyoddef bythoedd y ceugant :
cynghyd a phob cyflwr heb newidiaw : a rhoi gwell a newydd
ar bob peth, heb ei roi ar goll.

2555

Where'er you hear a naughty word,
A second like it will be heard.

Gnawd am air serth un arall.

2556

Greatest knowledge, greatest life,
Greatest power in God are rife ;
And he who doth the greatest own,
Must his possession have alone.

O dri anghenfod y mae Duw : sef y mwyaf parth bywyd, y mwyaf
parth gwybod, a'r mwyaf parth nerth ; ac nis gellir namyn un
o'r mwyaf ar unpeth.

2557

Three things will meet
Success complete :
Efforts clever, efforts great,
Efforts just appropriate.

Tri pheth a ddybryn llwyddiant : priodawl ymgais ; hywaith
ymgais ; ac anghyffredin ymgais.

2558

Where fear is found, there hate is near,
And fear but follows cause of fear.

Nid ofnawg ond dygasawg,
Nid ofn heb achaws.

2559

All steers and heifers in the spoil,
Repay the Chamberlain his toil.

Gwas ystafell a gaiff yr anneiredd ac yr enderigedd o'r anrhaith, a
ddycer o orwlad.—*Laws.*

PRINTED BY
SPOTTISWOODE AND CO., NEW-STREET SQUARE
LONDON